D1116625

Black Communists Speak on Scottsboro

Black Communists Speak on Scottsboro

A Documentary History

Edited by
Walter T. Howard

 TEMPLE UNIVERSITY PRESS
Philadelphia

To my family:
Virginia, Ian, Austin, and
Chris and Stephanie

Temple University Press
1601 North Broad Street
Philadelphia PA 19122
www.temple.edu/tempress

♾ The paper used in this publication meets the requirements of the American
National Standard for Information Sciences—Permanence of Paper for Printed
Library Materials, ANSI Z39.48-1992

Library of Congress Cataloging-in-Publication Data

Black Communists speak on Scottsboro: a documentary history/edited by
Walter T. Howard.
  p. cm.
  Includes bibliographical references and index.
  ISBN-13: 978-1-59213-597-4 (cloth: alk. paper)
  ISBN-10: 1-59213-597-8 (cloth: alk. paper)
1. Scottsboro Trial, Scottsboro, Ala., 1931.   2. African American
communists—History.   I. Howard, Walter T., 1951-
  KF224.S34B53 2008
  345.761'9502523—dc22
                     2007021039

2 4 6 8 9 7 5 3 1

Contents

Preface and Acknowledgments

lack Communists Speak on Scottsboro is an account of a
neglected chapter in the story of the Scottsboro saga.
The Alabama tragedy stands as a major event in North
American and international race relations history during the 20th
century. Understandably, then, many historians have written
about it. Few scholars, however, have focused in any meaningful
way on what African American Communists—who were inti-
mately involved in the case—had to say about the incident. The
voice of this segment of the African American community has
been ignored or distorted.

To be sure, the role of African American Communists in the
noted Scottsboro case cannot be ignored by any serious student
of American, Southern, or African American history. This book
attempts to validate this point of view.

I have tried to select black Communist voices from the mass
of primary source material that deals with Scottsboro. Several
African American radicals were in positions in the Party hierarchy
where they could speak meaningfully in terms of policy and
tactics. For example, William L. Patterson headed up the
International Labor Defense, the Party's legal auxiliary, during

much of the time that it dealt with Scottsboro. Likewise, B. D. Amis led the League of Struggle for Negro Rights during the early days of the episode. Further, Harry Haywood, chief theorist of the black self-determination policy, offered what was the Communist Party's most serious theoretical analysis of Scottsboro. Other black Communists, including James Ford, Eugene Gordon, Cyril Briggs, and Angelo Herndon, articulated important statements about many aspects of the case. What is more, Benjamin J. Davis, Jr., the eminent Harlem Communist, visited the Scottsboro youths in prison and reported on their welfare. He also worked with the Scottsboro parents during the decade.

This survey of the responses of African American Communists to the infamous Scottsboro tragedy in the 1930s draws on fresh, unpublished sources including Moscow documents. The holdings of the Russian State Archives of Social and Political History, formerly the Russian Center for the Preservation and Study of Documents of Contemporary History, are separated into a number of "fonds," or collections, that represent different kinds of organizational apparatus found in modern Russia, chiefly in the Soviet period. Research for this book concentrated primarily on one deposit, fond 515, documents of the U.S. Communist Party. Documents of the International Red Aid, the International Trade Union Committee of Negro Workers, the League of Struggle for Negro Rights, and statements by the Central Committee of the Communist Party of the United States (CPUSA) are found in fond 515. In regard to International Labor Defense, useful materials, including the *Labor Defender*, were found at the Schomburg Center for Research in Black Culture of the New York Public Library.

I incurred many debts in the preparation of this book. It would not have been possible without the help and cooperation of so many people of goodwill at many institutions. Three historians of American Communism, Edward Johanningsmeier, John Earl Haynes, and Vernon Pedersen, were helpful as I utilized material from the files of the CPUSA at the Library of Congress in Washington, D.C.

I want to thank all the accommodating librarians and archivists at the Schomburg Center for Research in Black Culture of the New York Public Library, New York University's Tamiment Institute, and Pennsylvania State University's Historical Collections and Labor Archives. Ann Diseroad, current director of the Interlibrary Loan Department at Bloomsburg University, rendered me invaluable services in locating and obtaining important material. Many thanks to my academic home, the history department at Bloomsburg University, especially chairperson William V. Hudon and Joyce Bielen. Thanks also to the staff of Temple University Press who helped in this project, especially to Micah B. Kleit, Elena Coler, and Michel Avery for their patience, encouragement, and guidance.

Finally, I dedicate this book to my family for their enduring love and inspiration, especially my wife Gini.

Introduction:
Background and Context

Southern law officers, on 25 March 1931, detained nine young African American males at a railroad stop in Paint Rock, Alabama, after hearing of a brawl between black and white youths on a freight train. In the process, they came across two white women, Ruby Bates and Victoria Price, who promptly accused the nine young blacks of raping them. Four of the so-called Scottsboro youths—Roy and Andy Wright, Eugene Williams, and Haywood Patterson—were from Chattanooga, Tennessee. The five others—Ozie Powell, Clarence Norris, Olen Montgomery, Charlie Weems, and Willie Roberson—hailed from various places in Georgia. The latter had met the others for the first time on the train. Olen Montgomery, wholly blind in one eye and nearly sightless in the other, as well as Willie Roberson, who could barely walk owing to untreated syphilis, seemed from the beginning to be unlikely perpetrators in this case. As events unfolded, an incompetent seventy-year-old Milo C. Moody was appointed as legal counsel for the defense. The local black community in Chattanooga pooled their financial resources and retained a local white attorney named Stephen R. Roddy to represent the defendants from their city. Following four separate trials in as many days in early April 1931, four discrete all-white juries in the small town of Scottsboro found eight of the defendants guilty of rape. Judge Alfred E. Hawkins immediately sentenced them to death. In the matter of the youngest defendant, Roy Wright (thirteen years old), the jury and the prosecution could not agree upon a sentence (execution or life imprisonment) so the case resulted in a mistrial.

From the beginning of this case, the American Communist Party (CPUSA) enthusiastically embraced the cause of the Scottsboro youths as the cause célèbre of racial injustice in the South during the 1930s.[1] Its crusade on behalf of the nine young African American defendants—falsely charged with the rape of two white women and then hastily and repeatedly sentenced to death—was, in fact, a response to an edict handed down by the Communist International (Comintern) a few years earlier to place the "Negro problem" near the top of its American domestic agenda. Many white Communists participated in the Scottsboro campaign; however, it was African American Party members who took the lead in carrying out the CPUSA response to the affair. Indeed, black Communists such as B. D. Amis and William Patterson led the Party's chief race auxiliaries, the League of Struggle for Negro Rights (LSNR) and the International Labor Defense (ILD), which handled the case on a day-to-day basis. Likewise, it was Harry Haywood and Patterson who were among the chief theorists about Scottsboro and the Party's racial policy at the time. George Padmore, a leader of the International Trade Union Committee of Negro Workers, helped to lead the international protest against Alabama's mistreatment of the Scottsboro defendants. Numerous other black Communists, including James Ford, Cyril Briggs and Eugene Gordon, wrote articles and essays in key publications about the entire matter and were particularly important in attacking the middle-class National Association for the Advancement of Colored People (NAACP) for its initial timidity in the case. And finally, it was African American Party member Benjamin Davis, Jr., who, for years, regularly visited the

Scottsboro youths in prison, monitored their treatment, and reported on the abuses they suffered at the hands of Alabama authorities.

Scholarship about the African American Left has evolved considerably over the last several decades. Before the 1980s, for example, most historians embraced a simplistic view of black Marxist history. The standard model held that the association between Communists and black militants was intrinsically fraudulent. The view that African American radicals predictably assumed a second-rate status under white Leninists can be traced back to historians and literary critics of the 1960s and 1970s.[2] In more recent years, however, specialists who focus on the Depression era, early to mid-twentieth century American radicalism, black Atlantic studies, and whiteness studies have witnessed the publication of important monographs that offer a new paradigm. The revisionist view of historians like Robin G. D. Kelley and Mark Naison is that black radicals were autonomous in their relationship to the CPUSA and the Comintern. Finding a middle ground between the two views of black Communists as either mindless dupes of the Soviet-dominated Comintern or independent radicals who shrewdly avoided foreign influence is Mark Solomon. He argues for a duality on the part of black Communists.[3] They kept one eye on Moscow directives and the other one on grassroots racial conditions in the United States. The tension between the two determined their thoughts and actions.[4]

Solomon's view may best describe the African American Communists of the 1930s who responded to Scottsboro. They acted as both loyal Communists, operating through Party channels as internationalists, and as black American radicals struggling against indigenous white supremacy. They were also a diverse group, ranging from West Indian radicals such as Briggs and Padmore, to well-educated attorneys such as Patterson and Davis, to homegrown black workers such Haywood, Ford and Amis. Some came from rural backgrounds, others from urban areas: Haywood descended from former slaves in Nebraska and Amis was mentored in Chicago by Ida B. Wells. The shared view of these assorted African American Communists asserted that black workers in America were exploited and oppressed more cruelly than any other group. Besides, they claimed, the history of Southern blacks could be characterized as essentially a reign of terror of slavery, segregation, disenfranchisement, lynching, persecution, rape, and murder. Black middle-class reform organizations such as the NAACP and the Urban League were too diffident and controlled by white elites. Further, because of the anti-black policies of organized labor, African American workers had given up on help from this source, and they had either been driven into the camp of labor's enemies, or had been compelled to develop purely racial organizations which sought solely racial aims. The Communist Party, they insisted, supported African Americans in their struggle for liberation, and helped them in their fight for economic, political, and social equality. It sought to completely destroy the barrier of race prejudice that had been used to keep black and white workers apart and bind them into a solid union of revolutionary forces for the overthrow of the common enemy. Black Communists were thinking along these lines when they encountered Scottsboro.[5]

The Road to Scottsboro

During the "Red Summer" of 1919, in the chaos that followed World War I and in the afterglow of the Russian Revolution, white radicals initiated the American Communist movement. Its birth was accompanied by an eruption of major race riots in the United States that signaled a new militant resistance by young blacks to American racial proscriptions. "New Negro" intellectuals gave voice to this militancy. Some of them, expressing solidarity with the pro-Bolshevik uprisings occurring in Europe at the time, were struck by Bolshevism's appeal not only to the working class of highly industrialized nations, but to oppressed national ethnic minorities.[6]

In spite of this interest, however, few blacks enlisted in the new radical movement. In the early years of the Communist Party's history in the United States, this new Marxist-Leninist organization claimed few African American members.[7] Most Party devotees came from foreign language federations formerly associated with the Socialist Party of America (SP). Moreover, these immigrant workers from Eastern and Southern Europe did not have much positive contact with black Americans.[8] The source of the negligence can indeed be traced to the Socialist Party. The SP had attracted few African Americans members in the years before 1919. True, Eugene Debs and other prominent Socialist leaders were usually opponents of racial segregation, disenfranchisement, peonage, and lynching. Nevertheless, American Socialists did not emphasize work with blacks and they often downplayed or ignored white supremacy in the form of their party's allegiance to trade unions that discriminated against non-white workers. Historians generally agree that the Socialist Party was unwilling to combat vigorously the racial inequities among American workers.[9]

Communists in the United States, like the Socialists, at first displayed only a slight concern with black workers. They also failed to engage the young black militants that emerged on the scene in the post-war period.[10] By the early 1920s, however, the American Communist Party defined the "Negro problem" in the United States in a global context. As an instrument of world revolution and anti-colonialism, the CPUSA approached the racial situation from that broad perspective. Accordingly, black Americans combating Jim Crow and lynching were essentially no different than Africans fighting for national independence and self-determination. Not surprisingly, then, the Party proved most attractive at this time to black laborers who displayed internationalist proclivities. In fact, a number of African American members of the CPUSA in the early 1920s were immigrant workers from the West Indies. Understandably, they viewed the struggles of the black working class in the United States in the larger context of non-Europeans fighting against capitalism and imperialism.[11]

During the middle of the 1920s some leaders of the African Blood Brotherhood (ABB), a black socialist organization that boasted a number of black Jamaican radicals in its ranks, linked up with the CPUSA. A black Marxist organization active during the Harlem Renaissance, the ABB was organized by the black radical journalist Cyril V. Briggs. The ABB also opposed American participation in WWI and linked the struggle for black liberation in the United States to the battle against European colonization in Africa. In 1918, Briggs also started a new magazine called the *Crusader*. The ABB backed the Socialist Party electoral campaigns of A. Philip Randolph and exposed lynchings in the South and job discrimination in the North. Briggs believed that the African American's true place was with labor and that blacks would benefit from the triumph of labor and the destruction of the "Capitol Civilization." A secret revolutionary organization, its purpose and program was the liberation of African people and the redemption of the African race. The program of the ABB emphasized racial pride, Black Nationalism, Pan-Africanism, and an economic analysis of the African American struggle which linked it to colonialism and imperialism. By 1925 the ABB leadership had established close ties with the Communist Party.[12]

During the early 1920s, the Soviets invited a small group of black Communists to Moscow, ostensibly for the purpose of preparing them for Party work in Africa. In the United States, however, the Party's focus on the issue of class rather than race acted so as to reduce the importance of so-called "Negro work." What is more, African American migrants who moved into Northern industrial centers were frequently utilized as strike-breakers by various industrialists. White Communists felt put off by this development. Subsequently, in the mid-1920s the CPUSA set up a particular organization for African American members, the American Negro Labor Congress (ANLC). Formed in Chicago in October 1925 under the auspices of the American Communist Party, the ANLC replaced earlier attempts by the CPUSA to organize black workers and leftists in the ABB. Its early leaders included Lovett Fort-Whiteman (national organizer),

H.V. Phillips (national secretary), as well as Harry Haywood. Black AFL workers had been scared off by the anticommunist baiting of AFL president William Green in the press. The program of ANLC called for the formation of "united fronts" in all centers of black population, with special emphasis on labor unions. Organizations composed of black and white workers were to be admitted, as were unorganized black workers. "Local councils" influenced by the ANCL were to facilitate, when possible, the end of racial discrimination in the AFL (Jim Crow locals) and other white labor organizations. The ANLC also supported equal pay for black workers, the anti-lynching movement, the end of racial segregation and political disfranchisement, and the end of all forms of industrial discrimination.

In spite of its worthwhile goals, some African Americans looked askance at the ANLC. Indeed, it often seemed to many to be little more than a Jim Crow auxiliary itself of the CPUSA. Additionally, its black members seemed to be assigned duties and activities that appeared to have little revolutionary importance.[13] Furthermore, the ANLC consistently attacked the NAACP and other similar black organizations as middle-class reformists controlled by white elites. Finally, the ANLC and the Party had a complicated relationship with the Universal Negro Improvement Association (UNIA) of Marcus Garvey. Even though the CPUSA approved of Garvey's encouragement of "race consciousness," it tenaciously opposed his back-to-Africa version of black nationalism. For his part, Garvey responded to Party recruiting within the ranks of the UNIA by expelling Communist sympathizers.[14]

Three years after the founding of the ANLC, everything changed drastically on the racial front. In 1928, the Sixth Congress of the Comintern changed Party policy spectacularly. Based on the old Leninist notion that oppressed ethnics within Czarist Russia should demand national self-determination, it asserted that by analogy African Americans in the United States comprised a separate nation.[15] Similarly, it claimed that black tenant farmers and sharecroppers in the southern regions were, in fact, an embryonic revolutionary group. The Comintern instructed American Communists to make the demand for a separate nation for African Americans within the South's "black belt" (the counties with a majority black population). As the Communists understood it, the black belt stretched from eastern Virginia and the Carolinas through central Georgia, Alabama, the delta regions of Mississippi and Louisiana and to the coastal areas of Texas. American Communists, black and white, adopted the new policy and moved forward to implement it.[16]

Other Leftist groups often ridiculed this new Communist policy as did many black reformers.[17] In any case, the Party soon found itself in a position where it was easier to support the goal of national self-determination for blacks in its theoretical writings than in its practical work. Still, during the late 1920s Communists sent organizers to the Deep South. For the most part, Party operatives in the region focused their work on the very concrete issues of organizing miners, steelworkers, and tenant farmers, as well as fighting against utility shutoffs, evictions, job discrimination, lynchings, and the pervasive system of Jim Crow.[18] As clearly shown by Columbia University historian Robin D. G. Kelley, black Communists in the South drew on the longstanding tradition of resistance to white authority to bolster Party work and objectives. Alabama Communists and their Share Croppers' Union, formed at this time, persisted in organizing marginalized rural black workers. They eventually claimed about eight thousand members after leading a strike in 1934 that resulted in higher wages for cotton pickers despite intense hostility from local whites.[19]

As an exercise in dialectics, American Communists sought to wed two opposing ideas: the fight for self-determination in the black belt and attempts at biracial organizing based on the guiding concept of class solidarity. Predictably, the Party's determined defense of black rights hindered its ability to recruit white Southerners. The Party's best known efforts to organize white workers and farmers during this time were in the textile workers' strike in Gastonia, North Carolina (1929) and in the coal strike in Harlan County, Kentucky (1931). In these episodes, the Communists' strong support for civil rights was always used against them to discourage whites from participating in biracial struggles. The few white Communists in the South who crossed the color line to work in black communities were usually ostracized by whites.[20] The Party, outside the South, also dealt with issues important to black Americans. It fought white supremacy on many fronts in the Depression decade. Party members led campaigns against poor housing and evictions, for unemployment relief, against police terror and lynching. Indeed, they organized mass struggles for the defense of victims of all kinds of unfair racial treatment. Communists even petitioned against the color line in baseball. In the social realm, they staged interracial meetings, socials, and dances as well as demonstrations and get-togethers in all regions of the nation. En route to Washington, D.C., to demonstrate for the freedom of the Scottsboro youths, the Communists stopped to visit eating establishments that refused to serve African Americans.[21]

As a result of all these enterprises, African American membership in the CPUSA mushroomed from two hundred members in 1930, less than 3 percent of the total, to seven thousand in 1938, over 9 percent. The percentage of black members in several cities was noticeably greater. In 1931 in Chicago, almost one-fourth of the city's two thousand members were African American. Because blacks made up about 11 percent of the total American population, these figures signify a moderate step forward in constructing a multiracial movement. Moreover, in Jim Crow America the CPUSA was one of the few integrated organizations in the country. The Communist Party also methodically developed and promoted black leaders through the ranks, beginning in 1929 by electing six African Americans to its central committee. It also picked black Party leader James Ford as its vice-presidential candidate in the elections of 1932 and 1936.[22]

Black Communists and Scottsboro

During the thirties, the most well known work by Communists in the South was their defense, through the League of Struggle for Negro Rights (LSNR) and the International Labor Defense (ILD), of the Scottsboro youths. These nine young black men were arrested in March of 1931 after a run-in with some white youths who were also riding the rails in search of employment. Subsequently, the black youths were convicted and sentenced to death on the charge of raping two white women who were also found on the same train. Indisputable medical evidence, however, clearly indicated their innocence.[23] [The state of Alabama belatedly issued formal pardons for the Scottsboro defendants in the 1970s.]

The CPUSA, the LSNR, and the ILD were the first to offer assistance. Black Communists, in particular, jumped on the Scottsboro case.[24] One way they expressed their keen interest was as Party leaders. For example, as a leader of the LSNR, B. D. Amis, fired off telegrams and letters to the Alabama governor, LSNR branches, and black newspaper editors, thus launching the campaign to save the Scottsboro victims.[25] Black Party leaders undoubtedly approved when the Central Committee of the CPUSA issued a statement on April 10, 1931, calling on black and white workers to unite and rally to the cause of the Scottsboro youths. However, they were skeptical when the Party press published a letter of support from William Pickens, field organizer for the NAACP, to illustrate how the Communists were leading the struggle and being backed at this time by such middle-class reform groups.[26]

On April 9, 1931, Alabama Judge E. A. Hawkins sentenced all the defendants but Roy Wright to die in the electric chair at the notorious Kilby Prison on July 10. From the beginning, black Communists played a critical role in publicizing and analyzing the Scottsboro case. In fact, the first such radical to write an essay about the affair was the articulate attorney William L. Patterson who was soon to assume leadership of the ILD. His first essay, "Judge Lynch Goes to Court," represented a black Marxist interpretation of the case that focused on class as the best way to understand the racial dynamics that underlie the entire matter. The first round of Scottsboro trials in 1933 were, in his view, simply "legal lynchings," and as such, class-based racial injustice.[27]

As the Scottsboro youths awaited the July 10 execution date, black Communists worked to save their lives. In the LSNR organ, *The Liberator*, Cyril Briggs' essay, "The Scottsboro Case and Nat Turner Centenary," compared the planned execution of the Scottsboro nine to Virginia justice for Nat Turner and his followers in the 1830s. In the same June issue of *The Liberator*, B. D. Amis published an article, "They Shall Not Die," that gave the Party campaign its slogan.[28] Communists, black and white, participated in a host of protests against the Scottsboro verdicts. On April 25, the first big Scottsboro parade in Harlem was disrupted by New York City law enforcement. In April, Mrs. Janie Patterson, Haywood Patterson's mother, arrived in New York to begin the national protest campaign. She spoke before a meeting of a thousand workers. On May 3, the first big Southern mass meeting was held in Chattanooga, Tennessee. On May 16, six thousand workers paraded in a Harlem Scottsboro demonstration; about a week later, a Scottsboro conference, attended by nineteen organizations, was held in Chattanooga. On the last day of May, the first All-Southern conference in Chattanooga was attended by two hundred delegates. Finally, on June 27, five thousand African American and white workers paraded through the streets of Harlem in a Scottsboro protest march.[29] Internationally, on June 9, Scottsboro protests took place before the United States Legation at Riga, Latvia. And a few weeks later, the scheduled executions were stayed pending an appeal to the Alabama Supreme Court. On July 3, about 150,000 German workers filled the Lustgarten in Berlin and heard Mrs. Ada Wright plead for the lives of her sons and the other Scottsboro defendants.[30]

Black Communists such as William Patterson placed the Scottsboro affair in an international context and analyzed how the Soviet Union and its treatment of minorities compared to the United States' handling of blacks. Patterson came out in July with "No Race Hatred in Workers' Russia." In this essay, he contrasted U.S. race problems as seen in Scottsboro with what he believed to be the successful way that the Soviet Union handled its ethnic minorities. He also compared Russian serfs with American slaves. He argued that the Communist Revolution in Russia of 1917 and its aftermath had brought the genuine right of self-determination to that nation's oppressed minorities, but the American Civil War still had not brought full liberation for the black minority of the United States.[31]

Black Communists in 1931 took part in international protests on behalf of the Scottsboro prisoners. In July, the International Trade Union Committee of Negro Workers in Hamburg, Germany, under the leadership of black Communist George Padmore, through its organ, *The Negro Worker*, called upon the international proletariat "to increase its vigilance, to increase its protests." Padmore, a future Pan-Africanist, was fearless in criticizing whites in and out of the Communist movement for acts of racial chauvinism. Likewise, at the CPUSA's Thirteenth Plenum in September 1931, B. D. Amis delivered a powerful twenty-minute speech in which he chastised white Communists for slighting the Scottsboro parents by having them wash dishes and clean house. This speech showed that black Communists were free to criticize the Party in regard to race.[32]

Between April and December 1931, the ILD and the NAACP battled for the right to represent the Scottsboro defendants. Many African American Communists tore into the NAACP. The attacks could be brutal, as the one advanced by black writer and Communist Eugene Gordon. In his article in the August issue of the ILD organ, the *Labor Defender*, "Scottsboro—And the Nice People," he ridiculed the hesitant middle-class black reform organization as the "Nice Association for the Advancement of Colored People." Gordon also related that at a recent Scottsboro meeting, NAACP Field Secretary William Pickens was challenged by a questioner in the audience: "Mr. Pickens, is it not true that at the beginning of the Scottsboro case you said you did not know why the NAACP was not doing anything, and is it not true that you contributed to the ILD to help defend these boys? Why are you attacking the ILD now?" Pickens was surprised and offered no credible answer to this telling inquiry.[33]

In January 1932 the CPUSA organ, the *Daily Worker*, published an appeal from the Scottsboro mothers that pulled at its readers' heartstrings. That same month Harry Haywood, a member of the Central Committee since October 1931, wrote a scathing piece for the ILD calling the NAACP an "assistant hangman." At the beginning of 1932, the NAACP at last withdrew from the case. A couple of months later, the Alabama Supreme Court, by a vote of 6-1, affirmed the convictions of seven of the youths. The conviction of Eugene Williams was reversed on the grounds that he was a juvenile under state law in 1931. In April 1932, the International Trade Union Committee of Negro Workers and George Padmore again entered the fray and issued an international protest of the scheduled execution of the Scottsboro defendants set for April 6, 1932. James W. Ford, the Party's most senior black Communist and vice-presidential candidate in 1932 and 1936, set the Scottsboro story once again in an international context with his essay, "Scottsboro Before the World," which appeared in the *Labor Defender* in April 1932.[34]

On April 19, 1932, the Alabama Supreme Court granted a stay of execution for the Scottsboro defendants until June 24. As the youths sat on death row, black Communist Eugene Gordon issued "A Call to Millions" to agitate and protest to save the lives of the "Scottsboro Nine." In May, however, the U.S. Supreme Court announced that it would review the cases. At this point, in the summer of 1932, Haywood assessed the entire affair in "Scottsboro and Beyond." He reminded his readers that

> in the midst of the intense, world-wide fight for the freedom of the Scottsboro victims, it is well to get a perspective view of the larger issue involved in the case. The Scottsboro frame-up is not an isolated instance of persecution; it is part

and parcel of a huge, cold-blooded system of oppression and terrorization of millions of Negro toilers, a system that has been well nigh reduced to a science by the boss class that imposes it."[35]

That same summer the ILD published a fascinating exchange of letters between Viola Montgomery and "Mother Mooney" [the ILD was also leading the crusade to free Tom Mooney from prison as a cause célèbre of class injustice]. Communists also published a story by a Scottsboro mother, Ada Wright, about her famous European tour of 1932. It was titled, "I Go to Jail for the Scottsboro Youths," and appeared in the *Labor Defender* in October. She stated, "Yes, I have been to prison in our struggle to save the Scottsboro boys. And, I will say now that I am willing to go again, and for a longer time if it will help the cause in which so many workers are struggling."[36]

On October 10 the Scottsboro appeal to the U.S. Supreme Court was argued by Walter H. Pollak, constitutional attorney retained by the ILD. Black Communist Cyril Briggs, in an essay, "Whose Supreme Court[?]," covered the Court hearing of the Scottsboro appeal in November 1932 and offered up a critical class analysis in anticipation of a negative decision. On the eve of the Supreme Court ruling, William Patterson published a "Manifesto to the Negro People" in the *Labor Defender* that described African Americans as victims of class terrorism in white America. He called on blacks of all classes to fight mob violence, lynching, and "Jim Crowism" in the American South by agitating for the defense of the Scottsboro youths. Black and white Communists alike were surprised when, in a successful appeal, the Supreme Court overturned the convictions. The court held in *Powell v. Alabama*, 287 U.S. 45 (1932), that the state of Alabama's failure to provide the defendants with adequate, competent counsel in a capital case violated their rights under the Fourteenth Amendment.[37]

Black Communist Harry Haywood, the self-proclaimed "black Bolshevik," and the Party's chief theorist in regard to self-determination and the black belt thesis, laid out a masterful analysis in *The Communist* in December 1932. He maintained that the Supreme Court decision vindicated "the correctness of the revolutionary policy of the Communist Party." He continued, "At the same time, the decision of the Supreme Court was calculated to revive the confidence of the masses in the bourgeois-democratic institutions." He summed up the Party's position that Scottsboro was an expression of the "national oppression of the Negro people," that revolutionary tactics not reformist efforts had saved the defendants' lives, that the Socialist Party was wrong to support the NAACP against the ILD in this case, and that the struggle to save the Scottsboro Nine was actually just beginning. In this analysis, Haywood went to great lengths to defend his "self-determination" theory against criticisms from Socialist Norman Thomas. He claimed in passionate language that the struggle for black rights in the "black belt" was at the heart of the black freedom movement in the United States.[38]

In January 1933, William Patterson offered a fully developed theoretical analysis of the Supreme Court decision. He viewed the tactical legal victory as an opportunity to advance a revolutionary agenda for black America, especially in the lynch-prone Southern black belt region. The mass appeal of the Scottsboro case and the anti-lynching campaign was a way to stimulate a revolutionary consciousness among powerless and marginalized African Americans in the South. Patterson, in fact, called Scottsboro "a revolutionary arsenal." In February, he plotted strategy and made ILD plans public in "Scottsboro—Our Next Tasks"; in March, he wrote for the Party, "We Indict the Alabama Lynchers." Samuel S. Liebowitz, noted New York criminal attorney, retained on March 23 by William Patterson, took charge of the defense. Patterson published an "Open Letter" in early March 1933 detailing just what the role of non-Communist lawyers, such as Liebowitz, was in the Scottsboro case. In April, the *Daily Worker* praised how well Patterson had handled the Scottsboro campaign.[39]

On March 27, a separation of the case of Haywood Patterson from that of the other defendants was secured by the ILD. He was placed on trial at Decatur in Morgan County before the venerable Judge James E. Horton. Ruby Bates, on April 7, came into court and testified for the defense. Originally a complaining witness, she reversed her previous testimony and denied the boys committed rape on her or Victoria Price. Price, however, repeated her original testimony. On April 9, the all-white Alabama jury convicted Patterson for the second time and again sentenced him to die in the electric chair.[40]

The ILD's Attorney Joseph R. Brodsky, in April 1933, filed a motion with Judge Horton for a new trial for Patterson on the grounds that the conviction was against the weight of the evidence. In the meantime, the Scottsboro defendants, on April 28, protested ill treatment in Jefferson County Jail, Birmingham, with a hunger strike. On May 5, in a mass Scottsboro march to Washington, D.C., black and white protesters carried a petition signed by 200,000 people that demanded freedom for the Scottsboro nine. On May 28, Ruby Bates joined a delegation to the White House headed by William Patterson. Vice President John N. Garner met with the delegation.[41] And about one month later, Judge Horton granted the motion for a new trial for Haywood Patterson and set aside the conviction with a lengthy opinion reviewing the case and concluding that the conviction was unjustified by the evidence. Horton believed that Price had lied on the witness stand. His decision elicited an international response from International Red Aid, the parent body for the ILD. It stated, "Executive Committee International Red Aid greets new trial [of] Patterson as [a] result [of the] mass effort organized by [the] International Labor Defense."[42]

On November 20, 1933, Patterson went on trial for the third time, this time before Judge William Washington Callahan, at Decatur. Three days later, the defense challenged the authenticity of seven African American names placed on the jury roll, charging forgery. On December 1, Patterson was convicted for the third time and again the death sentence was imposed. Clarence Norris was put on trial immediately afterwards and then convicted and similarly sentenced a week later. It was

Norris's second trial, his first, like that of the others, having been at Scottsboro. Liebowitz, Brodsky, and George W. Chamlee of Chattanooga represented both defendants.[43]

William Patterson immediately responded to these developments. In the *Labor Defender* in February 1934, he asserted in an essay titled, "Scottsboro Protest Must Grow," that "the second Decatur trial was a revelation to tens of thousands of white and Negro workers. The class character of American courts was made more clear." He also asserted in his analysis that "Judge Callahan has strikingly proven the correctness of the position of the International Labor Defense. The courts are one of the strongest weapons of the ruling class."[44] In April 1934, black Communist Benjamin Davis, a graduate of Harvard Law School, wrote Liebowitz and William Patterson letters reporting on the mistreatment of the Scottsboro defendants in jail. He related stories that ranged from physical abuse to psychological harassment to denial of access to legal counsel. Patterson immediately protested the maltreatment to Alabama authorities, who in turn ignored them. In the meantime, five Scottsboro mothers, accompanied by Ruby Bates, called at the White House on Mother's Day. President Franklin Roosevelt was out. Almost two weeks later, appeals in both cases were argued in the Alabama Supreme Court by Liebowitz and ILD attorney Osmond K. Fraenkel. The ILD, on June 23, mailed Roosevelt a complete documented statement on the case, demanding his intervention. Five days later, the Alabama Supreme Court affirmed the convictions.[45]

In 1935, the CPUSA, following the Comintern's lead, embraced a new policy of the united front designed to ally the Party with liberals, progressives, and socialists against fascism. African American Communists were swept up in this change in Party operations just as Liebowitz formed the American Scottsboro Committee (ASC). Further, on January 7, 1935, the United States Supreme Court granted petitions for review of the convictions of Patterson and Norris. From February 15 to 18, appeals were argued by Liebowitz of the ASC as well as Walter Pollak and Osmond Fraenkel of the ILD. The Supreme Court, on April 1, reversed the convictions of both defendants on the ground that African Americans were excluded from the panel of grand and petit jurors which indicted and tried them. Black Communists considered this Supreme Court decision an important tactical victory, but not the ultimate goal of their program.[46] In 1935, they looked on with dismay as Alabama prepared for more prosecution. On May 1, new warrants were sworn out by Victoria Price, the only complaining witness since the withdrawal of Ruby Bates. The grand jury at Scottsboro, on November 13, returned new indictments for rape against all the defendants. One African American citizen, Creed Conyer, sat on the grand jury for the first time in the memory of any resident of Alabama. A two-thirds vote was sufficient to return the indictment.[47]

As Communists pursued a united front strategy in 1935, they lost control of the Scottsboro defense, although they continued to publicize the case. Accordingly, African American Party members no longer played major roles in the way the affair was handled. In December 1935, the ASC was dissolved and the Scottsboro Defense Committee (SDC) was formed, composed of all groups then cooperating in the defense. The SDC was made up of representatives of the International Labor Defense, the National Association for the Advancement of Colored People, the American Civil Liberties Union, the Methodist Federation for Social Service, the League for Industrial Democracy, and the Church League for Industrial Democracy (Episcopal). The Scottsboro Defense Committee took over the legal defense, while the ILD continued its public campaign for the freedom of the nine. In the united front approach, African American Communists were marginalized in the case.[48]

Early in January 1936, the Scottsboro defendants pled not guilty at their arraignments. On January 20, Liebowitz, C. L. Watts, of Huntsville, Alabama, and Chamlee conducted Haywood Patterson's defense. Three days later he was convicted for the fourth time. Judge Callahan sentenced him to seventy-five years in prison. At this point a tragedy temporarily brought black Communists back into the case. The nine defendants, on

January 24, were on the way back to Birmingham jail. An incident occurred in the automobile of Sheriff J. Street Sandlin of Decatur. Ozie Powell slashed a deputy; Sandlin shot Powell. Benjamin Davis interviewed the youths and publicized this incident in the Communist press so as to tell the story from Powell's point of view.[49]

Black Communists, like everyone else who followed this case, knew that by 1936, the state of Alabama had grown tired of Scottsboro and the surrounding controversy. Stories to this effect appeared in the press. F. Raymond Daniels, a. *New York Times* reporter who had covered the affair since 1931, repeatedly reported on the possibility of a compromise. Neither black nor white Communists were fully satisfied with the terms of the compromise once it was in place. In 1937, the Alabama State Supreme Court confirmed Haywood Patterson's fourth sentence. In July of that year Clarence Norris, convicted for the third time, received the death sentence; Andrew Wright, ninety-nine years; and Charles Weems, seventy-five-years.[50] Authorities sentenced Ozie Powell, who pled guilty to the charge of assault with intent to murder, to twenty years in prison. However, the rape charge against Powell and the four others was dropped. The state of Alabama announced the release of Roy Wright, Olen Montgomery, Eugene Williams, and Willie Roberson. Authorities returned the others to prison. Four were free, five were not.[51]

It was African American Communist Benjamin Davis who took up the task in the second half of the 1930s of following through on the Party's participation in the Scottsboro case. He coordinated the meeting of the Scottsboro mothers and the four released youths in Harlem in July 1937. Davis also monitored and reported on the continuing legal struggle for the Scottsboro defendants still in Alabama prisons. The Scottsboro campaign was only one of several important ILD cases in the South. The ILD also defended Angelo Herndon, a black Communist activist sentenced to death by Georgia for sedition. Black Communists helped to defend Herndon who had advocated national self-determination for African American in the black belt. He also demanded retribution for lynching and real due process for black criminal defendants. Hernon wrote a 1937 pamphlet that summarized the Scottsboro case up to that point and expressed the mixed, complicated thoughts and emotions felt by many supporters of the defendants.[52]

Epilogue

During the late 1930s, as interest in the Scottsboro case waned, African American members of the Communist Party muted their call for a separate black state within the United States. Instead, they campaigned for the end of segregation, disenfranchisement, and lynching as part of a new platform that "Communism is twentieth century Americanism."[53] Popular Front Communists, black and white alike, continued to emphasize issues pertaining to African American workers even as they denounced lynching and other similar violent acts directed at blacks. Further, Communists joined with labor and civil rights groups to form the Southern Conference for Human Welfare, which campaigned for civil rights and socialism. The Party also tailored its campaign for unity against fascism to appeal to the African American community. This was most clearly seen in the case of its opposition to the Italian invasion of Ethiopia in 1935. Black Party members such as Harry Haywood also fought in the Spanish Civil War in the Abraham Lincoln Brigade. It was, in fact, the first American military force to include blacks and whites integrated on an equal basis and to employ black officers commanding white troops.[54]

Negotiations for the release of the five Scottsboro defendants still in prison continued throughout the late 1930s. In fact, the united front forces, including black radicals, sustained their agitation for the freedom of the Scottsboro victims into the 1940s. In light of the military conflict in Europe during World War II, the nation became preoccupied with the war effort and interest in Scottsboro virtually disappeared. The Scottsboro Defense Committee grew inactive. Its chairperson, Allan Knight Chalmers, maintained minimal contact with the International Labor Defense.

The ILD, for its part, sent a monthly sum to each Scottsboro defendant still imprisoned.[55] On January 8, 1944, Andrew Wright (30 years old) and Clarence Norris (32 years old), were paroled. Charles Weems (age 33) was paroled later. Norris, out nine months, was re-imprisoned as a parole violator. Let out again in 1947, Norris headed North. Wright was returned twice to prison as a parole violator. Authorities paroled Ozie Powell on June 16, 1946. He moved to Georgia.

In April 1947, the International Labor Defense merged with the National Federation for Constitutional Liberties and the Veterans Against Discrimination. Together they formed the Civil Rights Congress (CRC). The CRC, led by black radicals, continued contact with Haywood Patterson and Andrew Wright. On July 17, 1948, Haywood Patterson escaped from Kilby Prison. In June 1950 Andy Wright was paroled to New York. The FBI arrested Haywood Patterson in Detroit. In August 1952 Haywood Patterson died. In 1959 Roy Wright tragically committed suicide. In 1976 Alabama Governor George Wallace pardoned Clarence Norris. In 1989, the last of the Scottsboro youths, Clarence Norris, died.

All through the Scottsboro episode black Communists played major roles. All the important Party leaders of color, William Patterson, Harry Haywood, James Ford, Cyril Briggs, B. D. Amis, George Padmore, and Eugene Gordon among others wrote, spoke, and agitated as part of a concerted campaign to save the lives of the nine African American victims in the Scottsboro case. Their efforts indicate that they acted not only as members of the Communist Party of the United States, but also as indigenous black radicals who were responding to unique American racial conditions.

Notes

1. The best standard treatments of Scottsboro are, of course, Dan T. Carter, *Scottsboro: A Tragedy of the American South* (Baton Rouge: Louisiana State University Press, 1979); and James E. Goodman, *Stories of Scottsboro*

(New York: Pantheon Books, 1994). See also, Hugh T. Murray, Jr., "Changing America and the Changing Image of Scottsboro," *Phylon* 38 (1977), 82–92; and Carroll Van West, "Perpetuating the Myth of America: Scottsboro and Its Interpreters," *South Atlantic Quarterly* 80 (1981), 37–48. Also useful is Gerald Horne, *Powell v. Alabama: The Scottsboro Boys and American Justice* (New York: Franklin Watts, 1977); Clarence Norris, *The Last of the Scottsboro Boys* (New York: Putnam, 1979); and Haywood Patterson with Earl Conrad, *Scottsboro Boy* (New York: Collier Books, 1969).

2. Harold Cruse, *The Crisis of the Negro Intellectual* (New York: Morrow, 1967); Nathan Huggins, ed., *Voices from the Harlem Renaissance* (New York: Oxford University Press, 1976); and David L. Lewis, *When Harlem Was in Vogue* (New York: Vintage, 1981). A recent example of the view that black writers were manipulated by white Communists is Henry Louis Gates, Jr., *The Signifying Monkey: A Theory of Afro-American Literary Criticism* (New York: Oxford University Press, 1988). For the earliest accounts of this perspective, see Wilson Record, *The Negro and the Communist Party* (Chapel Hill: University of North Carolina Press, 1951); and William Anthony Nolan, *Communism Versus the Negro* (Chicago: H. Regnery Co., 1951).

3. Historians are fortunate that Solomon's research files can be found at New York University. The Mark Solomon and Robert Kaufman Research Files on African Americans and Communism, Tamiment Library/Robert F. Wagner Labor Archives; Elmer Holmes Bobst Library, 70 Washington Square South, New York, New York 10012, New York Universities Libraries [hereafter cited as Solomon and Kaufman Research Files, Tamiment, NYU]. See also, Robin D. G. Kelley, *Hammer and Hoe: Alabama Communists during the Great Depression* (Chapel Hill: University of North Carolina Press, 1990); Mark Naison, *Communists in Harlem during the Depression* (Urbana: University of Illinois Press, 1983); Mark Solomon, *The Cry Was Unity: Communists and African Americans, 1917–1936* (Jackson: University Press of Mississippi, 1998), xxxiii-iv.

4. Solomon, *The Cry Was* Unity, xxxiii-iv. See also, Barbara Foley, *Radical Representations: Politics and Form in U.S. Proletarian Fiction, 1929–1941* (Durham, NC: Duke University Press, 1993); James A. Miller, "African-American Writing of "the" 1930s: A Prologue" in Bill Mullen and Sherry Lee Linkon, eds., *Radical Revisions: Rereading 1930s Culture* (Urbana, IL: University of Illinois Press, 1996), 78–90; William J. Maxwell, *New Negro, Old Left: African-American Writing and Communism Between the Wars* (New York: Columbia University Press, 1999); Cedric J. Robinson, *Black Marxism: The Making of the Black Radical Tradition* (Chapel Hill: University of North Carolina Press, reprint, 2000).

5. An excellent account of the international aspects of Scottsboro is James A. Miller, Susan D. Pennybacker, and Eve Rosenhaft, "Mother Ada

Wright and the International Campaign to Free the Scottsboro Boys," *American Historical Review* 106 (April 2001), 387–430. See also, Edward Johanningsmeier, "Communists and Black Freedom Movements in South Africa and the U.S. 1919–1950," *Journal of Southern African Studies* 30, no. 1 (March 2004), 155–80.

6. Claude McKay, "Soviet Russia and the Negro," *Crisis* 27 (December 1923), 61–65; A. Mitchell Palmer, 1919 Investigation Activities of the Department of Justice, U.S. Senate, 66th Cong., 1st sess. S. Doc., vol. 12, no. 153.

7. Fraser M. Ottanelli, *The Communist Party of the United States: From the Depression to World War II* (New Brunswick: Rutgers University Press, 1991), 36; Theodore Draper, *American Communism and Soviet Russia* (New York: Vintage, 1960, 1986 reprint), 320. See also, Philip S. Foner and James S. Allen, eds., *American Communism and Black Americans: A Documentary History, 1919-1929* (Philadelphia: Temple University Press, 1987).

8. Theodore Draper, *The Roots of American Communism* (New York: Viking, 1957); James Cannon, *The First Ten Years of American Communism* (New York: Pathfinders Press, 1973), 16–19; and Roger Kanet, "The Comintern and the 'Negro Question': Communist Policy in the United States and Africa, 1921–1941," *Survey* [U.K.] 19, no. 4 (Autumn 1973), 87–122.

9. The best recent study of the Socialist Party's racial views and practices is Sally M. Miller, *Race, Ethnicity, and Gender in Early Twentieth-Century American Socialism* (New York and London: Garland Publishing, 1996). See also, James Weinstein, *The Decline of Socialism in America, 1919–1925* (New York: Vintage, 1969), 65–73; David Shannon, *The Socialist Party of America: A History* (New York: Macmillan, 1955), 50–53; Draper, *American Communism and Soviet Russia*, 319–332.

10. Oscar Berland, "The Emergence of the Communist Perspective on the 'Negro Question' in America, 1919–1931, Part One," *Science and Society* 63/64 (Winter 1999/2000), 411–33.

11. Perhaps the best analysis of this early development can be found in Kate A. Baldwin, *Beyond the Color Line and the Iron Curtain: Reading Encounters Between Black and Red, 1922–1963* (Durham, NC: Duke University Press, 2002). See also, Harvey Klehr, *The Heyday of American Communism: The Depression Decade* (New York: Basic Books, 1984), 324.

12. Otto Huiswood, "Speech to the Third International," *International Press Correspondent* 3, 5 January 1923, 14–16; Baldwin, *Beyond the Color Line*; Woodford McClellan, "Africans and Black Americans in the Comintern Schools, 1925–1934," *International Journal of African Historical Studies* 26, no. 2 (1993), 371–90; James Winston, *Holding Aloft the Banner of Ethiopia: Caribbean Radicalism in Early Twentieth-Century America*

(London, New York: Verso, 1998); and Daryl Russell Grigsby, *For the People: Black Socialists in the United States, Africa, and the Caribbean* (San Diego: Asante Publications, 1987).

13. Berland, "The Emergence of the Communist Perspective on the "Negro Question" in America," 429–30. See also, John L. Gardner, "African Americans in the Soviet Union in the 1920s and 1930s: The Development of Transcontinental Protest," *Western Journal of Black Studies* 23, no. 3 (1999), 190–200.

14. Mark Solomon, *The Cry Was Unity*, 64–65; B. D. Amis, "Lynch Justice at Work," 29; John W. Van Zanter, "Communist Theory and the American Negro Question," *Review of Politics* 29, no. 4 (1967), 435–56; and Henry Williams, *Black Response to the American Left: 1917-1929* (Princeton, NJ: Princeton University, 1973). See also, Hugh T. Murray, Jr.,, "The NAACP Versus the Communist Party: The Scottsboro Rape Cases, 1931–1932," *Phylon* 28, no. 3 (1967), 267–87; Wilson Record, *Race and Radicalism: The NAACP and the Communist Party in Conflict* (Ithaca, NY: Cornell University Press, 1964); Daniel Webster Wynn, *The NAACP Versus Negro Revolutionary Protest: A Comparative Study of the Effectiveness of Each Movement* (New York: Exposition Press, 1955); Harry Haywood, *The Road to Negro Liberation: The Tasks of the Communist Party in Winning Working Class Leadership of the Negro Liberation Struggles, and the Fight Against Reactionary Nationalist-Reformist Movements among the Negro People* (New York: Workers Library, 1934) and *Black Bolshevik: Autobiography of an Afro-American Communist* (Chicago: Liberator Press, 1978); Carol Anderson, "Bleached Souls and Red Negroes: the NAACP and Black Communists in the Early Cold War, 1948–1952," in William Henry Chafe, ed., *The Achievement of American Liberalism: The New Deal and Its Legacies* (New York: Columbia University Press, 2003).

15. On parallels between ethnic minorities in Russia and various racial minorities around the world, see CPUSA Papers, The Russian State Archives of Social and Political History (RGASPI) [hereafter cited as CPUSA Papers, Fond 515], Moscow, 515-1-2338. See also, Helene Carrere d'Encausse, *The Great Challenge, Nationalities and the Bolshevik State, 1917-1930* (New York: Holmes & Meier, 1991).

16. Harvey Klehr and William Tompson, "Self-Determination in the Black Belt: Origins of a Communist Policy," *Labor History* 30 (Summer 1989), 354–66.

17. Michael Rywkin, "Black Americans: A Race or Nationality? Some Communist Viewpoints," *Canadian Review of Studies in Nationalism* 3, no. 1 (1975), 55–77.

18. Tony Thomas, "Black Nationalism and Confused Marxists," *Black Scholar* 4, no. 1 (1972), 23–39.

19. Kelley, *Hammer and Hoe*, 99–101.

20. Bert Cochran, *Labor and Communism: The Conflict That Shaped American Unions* (Princeton: Princeton University Press, 1977); and Robert Gipe, *Which Side Are You Are On? The Harlan County Coal Miners, 1931–1931* (Urbana: University of Illinois Press, reprint edition, 2002).

21. Kelley, *Hammer and Hoe*; and Naison, *Communists in Harlem*.

22. R. J. Alperin, *Organization in the Communist Party, United States, 1931–1938*, PhD diss., Northwestern University, 1959, 49; and Paul D'Amato, "The Communist Party and Black Liberation in the 1930s," *International Socialist Review* 1 (Summer 1997), 1–12.

23. Notes, "Scottsboro, Ala.—Case," 1931, Library of Congress, NAACP Papers, Scottsboro Series, Microfilm Part 6.

24. In his autobiography, Harry Haywood relates that he, Sol Harper, and B. D. Amis were the three black Communists who went to Earl Browder's office to initiate the CPUSA's Scottsboro campaign. Haywood, *Black Bolshevik*, 360–61.

25. Telegram from Executive Committee of the LSNR to Governor B. M. Miller, April 9, 1931; Negro Department Central Committee to LSNR Affiliates, April 9, 1931; Editor of *The Liberator* to Negro Editors, April 21, 1931, CPUSA Papers, Moscow, Fond 515-1-2222, 2339; Interview of B. D. Amis by Barry Amis, July 24–26, 1988, transcripts in possession of Amis family and shared with the author.

26. *Daily Worker*, April 19, 1931.

27. William L. Patterson, "Judge Lynch Goes to Court," *Labor Defender*, May 1931; and Haywood, *Black Bolshevik*, 362–63.

28. Cyril Briggs, "The Scottsboro Case and the Nat Turner Centenary," *The Liberator*, June 6, 1931; and B. D. Amis, "They Shall Not Die!" ibid.

29. *Daily Worker*, April 17, 18, 1931; Carter, *Scottsboro*, 49–59; Murray, "The NAACP versus the Communist Party," 278; James S. Allen, "Scottsboro—A Proclamation of Freedom," *Labor Defender*, June 1935; Kelley, *Hammer and Hoe*, 78-79; and William L. Patterson, *The Man Who Cried Genocide: An Autobiography* (New York: International Publishers, 1971), 126–138.

30. Miller, Pennybacker, and Rosenhaft, "Mother Ada Wright and the International Campaign to Free the Scottsboro Boys," 387–430.

31. William L. Patterson, "No Race Hatred in Workers' Russia," *Labor Defender*, July 1931.

32. George Padmore, "Increase and Spread the Scottsboro Defense," *Negro Worker*, July 1931; and Negro Bureau of the Comintern, B. D. Amis speech at the 13th Plenum, CPUSA, September 1931, CPUSA Papers, Moscow, Fond 515. Author's interview with Debbie Amis Bell and Barry D.

Amis [daughter and son of B. D. Amis], November 4, 2005, Philadelphia, PA. See also, James R. Hooker, *Black Revolutionary: George Padmore's Path from Communism to Pan-Africanism* (New York: Praeger, 1967).

33. Eugene Gordon, "Scottsboro—And the Nice People," *Labor Defender*, August 1931.

34. *Daily Worker*, January 21, 1932; Harry Haywood, *Labor Defender*, January 1932; Executive Committee of International Red Aid statement, April 1932, CPUSA Papers, Moscow, Fond 515; James W. Ford, "Scottsboro Before the World," *Labor Defender*, April 1932. See also, Haywood, *Black Bolshevik*, 374–75.

35. Eugene Gordon, "A Call to Millions," *Labor Defender*, June 1932 and Harry Haywood, "Scottsboro and Beyond," ibid.

36. For the letter exchange between Viola Montgomery and Mother Mooney, see *Labor Defender*, June 1932 and Ada Wright, "I Go To Jail for the Scottsboro Boys," ibid., October 1932.

37. Cyril Briggs, "Whose Supreme Court?" *Labor Defender*, November 1932; and William L. Patterson, "Manifesto to the Negro People," ibid.

38. Harry Haywood, "The Scottsboro Decision: Victory of Revolutionary Struggle Over Reformist Betrayal," *The Communist*, December 1932. See also, Haywood, *Black Bolshevik*, 374–78.

39. Patterson, "The Scottsboro Decision: An Analysis, January 1933," Records of the International Labor Defense, Schomburg Center for Research in Black Culture, New York Public Library; Patterson, "Scottsboro—Our Next Tasks," *Labor Defender*, February 1933; Patterson, "We Indict the Alabama Lynchers," ibid., March 1933; "Open Letter from William L. Patterson, ILD Secretary,"nd, Records of the ILD, Schomburg Center, New York Public Library; *Daily Worker*, April 19, 1933.

40. Kelley, *Hammer and Hoe*, 86; Carter, *Scottsboro*, 181–82, 186, 191–234.

41. Scottsboro Trial—newspaper clippings, Box 2, Folder 28, Solomon and Kaufman Research Files, Tamiment, NYU.

42. Telegram from International Red Aid to ILD., June 23, 1933, CPUSA Papers, Moscow, Fond 515.

43. Scottsboro Trial—newspaper clippings, Box 2, Folder 28, Solomon and Kaufman Research Files, Tamiment, NYU; Kelley, *Hammer and Hoe*, 89; and Carter, *Scottsboro*, 268–70.

44. William L. Patterson, "Scottsboro Protest Must Grow," *Labor Defender*, February 1934.

45. Benjamin Davis to Samuel Liebowitz and William L. Patterson, April 1934, and telegram from ILD to Governor B. M. Miller, April 11, 1934, Records of the ILD, Schomburg Center, New York Public Library; Foner and Shapiro, *American Communism and Black Americans*, 249–319.

46. Carter, *Scottsboro*, 319–24; and Gerald Horne, *Black Liberation/Red Scare: Ben Davis and the Communist Party* (Newark: University of Delaware Press, 1994), 47–54. See also, Scottsboro Trial—newspaper clippings, Box 2, Folder 28, Solomon and Kaufman Research Files, Tamiment, NYU.

47. Carter, *Scottsboro*, 339; and Scottsboro Trial—newspaper clippings, Box 2, Folder 28, Solomon and Kaufman Research Files, Tamiment, NYU.

48. Patterson, *The Man Who Cried Genocide*, 126–138.

49. Scottsboro Trial—newspaper clippings, Box 2, Folder 28, Solomon and Kaufman Research Files, Tamiment, NYU. See also, Foner and Shapiro, *American Communism and Black Americans*, 249–319.

50. Carter, *Scottsboro*, 330–39; and Nell Irvin Painter, *A Narrative of Hosea Hudson: His Life as a Negro Communist in the South* (Cambridge: Harvard University Press, 1981), 83–88, 100–101, 138–45.

51. Carter, *Scottsboro*, 330-39. See also, Irving Howe and Lewis Coser, *The American Communist Party: A Critical History* (Boston: Beacon Press, 1957), 214–16.

52. Benjamin Davis, "2 Scottsboro Mothers Urge Fight for Boys," *Daily Worker*, July 30, 1937; Davis, "Scottsboro Appeal Filed in Alabama Defense Committee, ibid., August 6, 1937; Davis, "Jailed Scottsboro Boys are Menaced by Prison Sickness," ibid., September 9, 1937; and Herndon, *The Scottsboro Boys* (New York: Workers' Library, 1937). See also, Horne, *Ben Davis and the Communist Party*, 47–54; and Scottsboro Trial—newspaper clippings, Box 2, Folder 28, Solomon and Kaufman Research Files, Tamiment, NYU. For Herndon, see, Charles Martin, *The Angelo Herndon Case and Southern Justice* (Baton Rouge: Louisiana State University Press, 1976).

53. Naison, *Communists in Harlem*; and James W. Ford, "The United Front in the Field of Negro Work," *The Communist*, 14 (1935), 166.

54. Kelley, *Hammer and Hoe*, 214–26; Klehr, *Heyday of American Communism*, 345-47; Cicero Hughes, "Toward a Black United Front: The National Negro Congress Movement," PhD diss., Ohio University, 1982, 91–93.

55. Carter, *Scottsboro*, 319–46.

"They Shall Not Die!"

Fond 515, Files of the Communist Party of the United States in the Comintern Archives

Telegram from Executive Committee of League of Struggle for Negro Rights to Governor B. M. Miller of Alabama

April 9, 1931

The League of Struggle for Negro Rights vigorously protests the deliberate frame-up against the nine Negro youths and their railroading to the electric chair. This organization of ten thousand membership demands that you stop this legal lynching and holds you responsible to stay the hands of the lynch mob.

EXECUTIVE COMMITTEE
LEAGUE OF STRUGGLE FOR NEGRO RIGHTS
B. D. AMIS, PRESIDENT.

Fond 515, Files of the Communist Party of the United States in the Comintern Archives.

Statement by the Central Committee, Communist Party U.S.A.

April 9, 1931.

The Communist Party of the United States calls upon the white workers of Alabama, the white workers of the whole south and the whole United States to make the cause of the Negro workers their own cause. We call upon both Negro and white workers to unite and to rally to the cause of these 9 Negro boys who are being lynched in Scottsboro.

The Communist Party calls upon all working class and Negro organizations to adopt strong resolutions of protest, and to wire these to the governor of Alabama and to the Daily Worker. But wires to such capitalist officials alone will do no good, you must organize at the greatest possible speed mass meetings and militant mass demonstrations against this crime. Let the southern ruling class know that the working class will not tolerate further continuance of their bloody crimes against our class!

Certain "reformist" organizations, claiming to represent the interest of the Negroes, such as the National Association for the Advancement of Colored People, the Universal Negro Improvement Association, the Urban League, etc., are, in fact under the leadership and control of middle class reformists who, we are perfectly aware, cannot be depended upon to rally those organizations in defense of these helpless boys of Scottsboro. These reformist leaders can be expected, as usual, only to betray the Negro masses, and in this case it is easy to betray by pretending to believe that these boys are getting a "legal trial," whereas these reformists claim only to be "against illegal lynching." The Communist Party calls upon the rank and file members of these organizations nevertheless to give their support to the campaign to save these defenseless Negro boys.

We demand a united front of all working and farming masses of this country to stop the legal lynching at Scottsboro.

Workers, black and white——organize monster mass meetings, militant demonstrations! Let the southern ruling class know that we will tolerate their crimes against our class and the persecuted Negro race no longer!

The death penalty for lynchers! Stop the legal lynching at Scottsboro!

The Communists organized and inspired protests against the Scottsboro trials and sentences. The letter below, from William Pickens of the NAACP, reveals that at the beginning of the case even this black middle-class reform organization seemed to be following the Communist lead.

Daily Worker

April 19, 1931

Kansas City, Mo.

Dear Daily Worker:

I am writing from Kansas City, where I have just seen a copy of The Daily Worker for April 16th and noted the fight which the workers are making, thru I.L.D., to prevent the judicial massacre of Negro Youth in Alabama.

Enclosed is a small check for that cause. Please send it to I.L.D in enclosed stamp envelope.

The promptness with which the white workers have moved toward defending these helpless and innocent Negro boys, sons of black workers, is significant and prophetic. The only ultimate salvation for black and white workers is in their united defense, one of the other. Other causes and movements may do good work, but all other causes are good only as preliminaries to that consummation. The one objective for final security is the absolute and unqualified unity and cooperation of ALL WORKERS of all the exploited masses, across all race and color lines and all other lines.

In the present case the Daily Worker and the workers have moved, so far, more speedily and affectively than all other agencies put together. If you do not prevent Alabama from committing these horrible murders, you will at least educate working people, white and black, to the danger of division and the need of the union. In either event it will be a victory for the workers.

Enclosed is an article which I had written on the mere "probabilities" of the case when I received the first few meager details thru the lying daily press. They gave details but that was the only way, out of my experiences as a southern Negro, that I could make sanity out of the madness. I see the reports of the investigations of the workers' agents that I was not so far wrong, not wrong at all in the conclusion that these children are innocent and that they were framed.

This is one occasion for every Negro who has intelligence enough to read, to send aid to you and to I.L.D.

Very sincerely yours,

William Pickens

Fond 515, Files of the Communist Party of the United States in the Comintern Archives

Negro Department C. C.
P.O. Box 87, Station D.
New York, N.Y.
April 9, 1931

Dear Comrades:

The Central Committee instructs you to immediately arrange a series of mass protest meetings against the legal lynching of the 9 Negro youths in Scottsboro, Alabama.

The District Committee is responsible to initiate this campaign. These meetings must be held in every section of the districts. Large mass meetings of Negro and white workers, native and foreign-born must be mobilized for active participation in raising a huge protest against the ruling landlords and capitalists and their court, linking up this specific case with our preparations for May Day.

Lynchings must be a central figure in the May Day demonstrations. The local persecutions of Negro and white workers must likewise be closely connected with this latest outburst of terrorism.

The steps to be taken in this campaign are as follows:

1. The Party organizations to initiate the campaign.
2. The L.S.N.R. to make official calls for united fronts to all mass organizations, Negro organizations, clubs, fraternal orders, etc.
3. The YCL must likewise issue a call to all youth and sport clubs.
4. Each organization to hold protest meetings adopting protest resolutions and to send telegrams of protest to Governor Miller of Alabama.
5. The legal lynching of these 9 Negro youths must be a central figure in our preparations for May First.
6. Organizational gains, must be achieved to build the Liberator and the L.S.N.R.

Immediate response must be made as to what steps you are taking to carry through these instructions. When all arrangements are under way, report fully what they are.

Resolutions of meetings must immediately, at the conclusion of the demonstrations, be communicated to the Central Office and the Daily Worker.

All organizations especially Negro organizations must be visited and their sentiment aroused against this terror. Each must be stirred up and urged to hold protest meetings and send protest resolutions and telegrams to the state government.

You are to make the mass character of the demonstration the center of your reliance. These must be conducted with a view to continuing the movement and repeating the demonstrations on a mounting scale of mass participation.

Comradely your.

B.D. Amis

FOR THE CENTRAL COMMITTEE

Fond 515, Files of the Communist Party of the United States in the Comintern Archives

The Liberator

799 Broadway, Room 338
New York City
April 21, 1931

Dear Editor:

We write to you most urgently to draw your attention to the necessity of using the full power of the Negro press to defeat one of the worst crimes against our people that has ever been produced in the backward regions of the South. You are doubtless aware that at Scottsboro, Alabama, 9 Negro boys, ranging from 14 to 20 years of age, have recently been jammed through a hasty mock trial in a courthouse surrounded by a mob of ten thousand howling whites, and 8 of them were tried and sentenced to death in the electric chair within a space of four days.

In my joint capacity as editor of the Liberator and an official of the League of Struggle for Negro Rights, I have been working hard to get at the facts, have been in touch with other organizations and leaders, and, together with these, have succeeded in getting two attorneys from New York to go down to Birmingham, Alabama, where these lawyers have gotten into the jail and have seen the 8 boys who are sentenced to death. The facts we learned from them are in main points that follow:

1. They are typical honest and innocent hardworking lads of tender age and absolutely not of the hardened sort that could possibly be conceived to have committed the crime of violent attack upon women.

2. These boys, who are too simple and direct, as well as too young to be able to dissimulate under the pressure of a case of this kind, have told our attorneys a perfectly straightforward story accounting for their moves and everything that could possibly bear upon the case, and our attorneys assure us that there is not

the slightest doubt that the boys are telling the truth—that they had absolutely nothing to do with the affair and had never been near the women at all.

3. Their so-called "trial" was nothing less than the first act of a lynching, jammed through in almost the same number of hours that it would have required to perform the usual style of lynching under a tree in the open. They had no defense whatever that is worthy of mention.

4. Their so-called attorneys, according to our best information, were appointed by the court after the attorneys had openly expressed their desire to see the boys executed.

5. Everyone concerned in the case sneeringly regarded it as only a variation of the ordinary lynching; it being openly told to the howling mob outside that they could be assured it was unnecessary for them to hang the boys because the trial would be "almost as quick, and with the same results."

6. The boys (8 of them) stand condemned to die on July 10th. The 9th boy is being held back on some technical grounds for another trial.

7. The attorneys who were engaged by the International Labor Defense, New York City, in cooperation with us, have taken the first steps for an appeal, and from every legal aspect they would have every reason to expect success if it were possible for a colored man or even 9 colored children to receive a square deal from the "white supremacy" courts of Alabama.

8. However, the whole case shows itself to be a question of mass pressure. The background of the case is a terrible economic situation in that section of Alabama, where the colored farmers (share-croppers and tenants), and the white share-croppers and tenant farmers of the same class, have been having a great deal of friction with the white landlords. There is quite a movement against the usual gouging of the tenants and even a

certain tendency for the white tenants and the Negro tenants to make common cause against the landlords.

You will doubtless have noticed as well that the Southern white ruling class newspapers have recently been trying to stir up every possible hysteria against the race, doubtless being influenced more or less by the desire to start the fight between whites and blacks of the same class in order to divert the pressure from this case. The great unemployment of that section has added to the electricity in the air, especially as starving unemployed workers, black and white are actually organizing unemployed councils together, with no color line. Only a few days ago, for instance, the Ku Klux Klan attempted to break up with violence an unemployed council of Negroes and Whites at Greenville, S.C., where conditions are much the same.

It is my belief that the horrible tragedy which is now about to take place in the death of these boys on July 10th is a challenge which every Negro in America and the whole world must take up and fight out to the last ditch. I believe that if we can save these boys, this one act alone will give new courage to our people and will help immensely to turn the tide against the lynching of our people.

But as I said, it is a question of mass pressure. I am one of those who believes that we ourselves can exercise mass pressure in a case so horrible as the present one. It would be impossible to imagine a case where there is so much reason to fight.

Will the Negro press arise to this occasion and fight as one man to save those innocent boys?

I must urgently request you to throw your paper into this fight to save these boys. I believe the facts are before you. We have received rather extensive stories from the Crusader News Service to which I believe you also subscribe. Also, the Liberator will gladly cooperate in any way requested.

But I urge you to be quick about it! It takes time to get a real mass movement under way. We have already had conferences with various organizations, including Communists, trade unions, working men's clubs, etc., and others, and it has already been arranged that a demonstration on a large scale will take place on the first day of May in every city in the United States. Arrangements are being made to hold these demonstrations in the Southern cities as well as the Northern, such as Birmingham, Atlanta, Tampa, New Orleans, Chattanooga, and San Antonio. Our belief is that it is necessary to get thousands of our people into these demonstrations with banners inscribed with the demand to stop the legal lynching of these Negro boys at Scottsboro.

We most earnestly hope that you will respond to this request.

Sincerely yours,

B.D. Amis

EDITOR, THE LIBERATOR

Records of the International Labor Defense, Schomburg Center for Research in Black Culture, New York Public Library

"Judge Lynch Goes to Court"

Labor Defender

May 1931

William L. Patterson

Judge Lynch has put aside his noose, mask and gasoline for the moment—and returned to the courthouse.

Nine Negro workers were sentenced to death in almost as many hours by the state of Alabama. The oldest is 20. The ruling class does not care at this time to allow so large a group to be handled "out of court" by an unauthorized lynching committee. The state itself has taken the matter in hand. A bloody holiday is being "legally" prepared by the "duly" appointed authorities of Alabama at Scottsboro. They used to call such things "Roman holidays." Now it's typically American. The age-old cry of "rape" has been raised by the bosses to justify the masked terror of their court. But the mask is ill-adjusted. This viciousness of the master class looms forth unmistakably clear.

The bosses' court has chosen the "defense" lawyers for these Negro workers. These attorneys stated before the preliminary holiday preparations—the trial—that the "niggers ought to roast in the chair." The armed forces of the lynchers, the militia was called out to "protect" the nine workers.

The Negro workers were guilty of seeking work during a period when it was more profitable for the bosses to starve the workers than to give them employment. They "hopped" a freight train bound for Scottsboro where they heard work might be secured. In the car the Negro workers grabbed were seven white workers and two white women dressed in overalls.

These workers were also unemployed workers, the victims also of the bosses' insane form of government with its rewards to the workers of mass unemployment, starvation, sickness without insurance, prostitution, bloody wars and death.

But these white workers had learned from the lips of the bosses themselves the great hoax of the ruling class—the legend of "white supremacy." To them reared in the boss created atmosphere of race hatred bolstered by privileges of lynching, mob violence and indiscriminate terrorizing of Negroes, this myth of white supremacy seemed real. 10,000,000 white, starving unemployed workers also "proves" white supremacy.

The box car occupied by white workers was too good for "niggers." But the black workers fought for their lives. The girls were injured in the struggle—but not touched otherwise. The white workers telegraphed ahead their version of the affair and the bosses' police waited for the train to reach Scottsboro while the bosses' press whipped the town into lynch frenzy with its big headlined story of the "attack" by "nine burly black brutes" upon two white girls. A doctor's examination of the girls proved conclusively that they had not recently been touched sexually. Of course the vicious Negro baiting press of the landlord class concealed this fact.

Condemned to death, the Negro youths revolted in prison and fought with the guards until they were beaten unconscious.

The International Labor Defense has already sent two lawyers to the South to represent the boys. Mass protest is being raised by white and Negro workers all over America.

For white and black workers are rising in revolt against the bosses' civilization of profits in the ranks of the working class. In Arkansas white and black workers together broke in the padlocked warehouses of the landlords and took food for their starving wives and children. The spectre of a united front of white and black workers against white supremacy looms like a giant threat before the trembling throne of the bosses.

On May Day, the First of May, the white and black workers will demonstrate against the rising terror of the bosses and their policy of divide and rule. Lynching is part and parcel of the bosses' government of starvation and death.

An armed volunteer guard of Negro and white workers to defend these prisoners against lynchers! Death to the lynchers!

Fond 515, Files of the Communist Party of the United States in the Comintern Archives

"The Scottsboro Case and the Nat Turner Centenary"

The Liberator

June 6, 1931

Cyril Briggs

This coming November 11, 1931, will mark the one hundredth anniversary of the murder by the State of Virginia of the heroic Negro revolutionary, Nat Turner.

Not many Negro workers know about Nat Turner and the scores of other brave leaders of the numerous slave insurrections which constantly challenged the brutal power of the slave-owners and kept them constantly in fear and trembling.

Traitors Soft Peddle Revolutionary Traditions

The American bosses, with the support of the treacherous Negro petty bourgeois misleaders (preachers, landlords, businessmen, etc.) have nearly succeeded in wiping out of the consciousness of the Negro masses all memory of their glorious revolutionary traditions; for the bosses, whose oppression of the Negro masses is today as brutal as under chattel slavery, do not wish the exploited Negro masses to have any traditions of revolt and struggle against their oppressors. Such traditions would serve to stiffen their resistance to present-day share cropper slavery, lynching, etc., and would make it unpleasant for the bosses. In this, the bosses are ably seconded by the Negro Uncle Tom reformists who constantly try to stifle the protests of the Negro masses, as so clearly evidenced today in the Scottsboro case where reformist organizations and papers like N.A.A.C.P., the Chattanooga Ministers Alliance, the *Pittsburgh Courier*, etc., are trying their best to stop the nationwide mass protest against the outrageous frame-up and planned legal murder of nine Negro children.

Set Up Servile Example

In the effort to develop a slave psychology in the Negro masses, the American bosses and their Negro tools have done their best to kill the revolutionary traditions of the Negro masses. In place of such heroic figures as Nat Turner, Frederick Douglass, Denmark Vessey, etc., the white ruling class and their despicable agents within the Negro race have set up instead the servile figures of Booker T. Washington and the even more despicable Moton.

In support of this policy, the utmost care is taken by the prostitute bourgeois historians to consistently present the picture of the Negro as a slave, immemorially servile and subordinate, satisfied with his slave status and incapable of revolt. This boss policy is faithfully supported by the misleaders like Kelly Miller, the leadership of the N.A.A.C.P., the Urban League and other reformist organizations.

Misleaders Aid Murder of Boys

To these misleaders any thought of the frightfully oppressed Negro masses joining ranks with the revolutionary white workers in the fight against their common oppressor is unthinkable and horrible. That is why the leaders of the N.A.A.C.P., the Chattanooga Ministers Alliance and other Uncle Tom reformists are today opposing with every weapon at their command the united front of white and Negro workers to save the nine innocent Scottsboro Negro children. To these shameful misleaders it is preferable that these innocent children are murdered than that the Negro masses should smash through the barriers of Jim Crow isolation and join the white workers in a fighting alliance against the capitalist starvation system with its murderous lynch terror against the Negro masses.

The centenary of the murder of Nat Turner must be made the occasion for reviving the revolutionary traditions of the Negro masses, and for smashing the treacherous influence of the Uncle Tom reformists. Nat Turner Centenary memorial meetings must be held throughout the country on November 11. Hundreds of thousands of Negro and white workers must be made acquainted with the daring insurrection launched by Nat Turner against the Virginia slave power, and with his heroism on the scaffold to which he was condemned by the government of Virginia.

In order to make the Nat Turner Centenary a nationwide event and to draw in the largest possible masses, the League of Struggle for Negro Rights should at once take up the question of organizing the widest possible united front basis. For this purpose it is necessary that the National Committee of the L.S.N.R. should at once get busy on the task of drawing up a plan and sending out instructions to the various groups and affiliated bodies of the L.S.N.R. The time is already short if we are to mobilize a real mass celebration that will draw in hundreds of organizations and wide masses of Negro and white workers and poor farmers.

The Nat Turner Centenary meetings can be very effectively connected up with the Scottsboro campaign and made to serve as a further mobilization base for the fight to stop the legal lynching of the nine Alabama boys and to smash the system of boss oppression and lynching.

Fond 515, Files of the Communist Party of the United States in the Comintern Archives

"They Shall Not Die!"

The Liberator

June 6, 1931

B. D. Amis,

Millions of workers, colored and white, have been mobilized in the mass campaign conducted by the International Labor Defense (I.L.D.) and the League of Struggle for Negro Rights (L.S.N.R.) to save the lives of the nine innocent Negro children today facing the electric chair in the State of Alabama. Throughout the country the masses are thundering the battle-cry, THEY SHALL NOT DIE!

In thousands of meetings, in hundreds of protest parades and demonstrations, battling the bosses' police who would stifle their protest against this frightful legal murder, in scores of United Front Scottsboro Defense Conferences, in increasing financial support of the defense campaign, millions of white and Negro workers have demonstrated their indignation against the murderous court room lynching planned by the Southern boss lynchers. Everywhere, both North and South, the masses are rallying to the fight against this hideous railroading to the electric chair of nine innocent boys on the trumped-up charge of "rape" against two notorious white prostitutes. Everywhere, the determined cry is being raised, THEY SHALL NOT DIE!

North and South, white and colored workers, smashing through the boss-erected barriers of race prejudice and Jim-Crowism are forcing a mighty fighting alliance to save and free these boys. A fighting alliance that says to the bloody fascist bosses, THEY SHALL NOT DIE!

And at this spectacle of the growing unity of white and black workers the imperialist bosses are becoming increasingly alarmed. The organ of the fiendish Scottsboro lynchers, the Jackson County *Sentinel*, shrieks that the mass movement to save the nine boys is:

". . . THE MOST DANGEROUS MOVEMENT LAUNCHED IN THE SOUTH IN MANY YEARS!"

And the workers thunder back the fighting slogan: "THEY SHALL NOT DIE!"

This unity of the working-class, colored and white, is recognized by the bosses as a threat not only to the plans for the legal lynching of these nine youths but as a threat against the whole murderous system of Negro oppression and enslavement, against the capitalist hunger system! And the bosses are scared by that thunderous roar from the working-class, THEY SHALL NOT DIE!

This alarm of the southern boss lynchers is shared by the Negro tools and apologists of imperialism whose business of "uplifting," "advancement" (and other terms which cover up their robbery and betrayal of the Negro masses) thrives on the segregation and Jim Crowism enforced by the bosses. And they see this segregation crumbling before the advancing unity of the Negro and white masses. Thus the mass movement to save the nine boys is also seen as a dangerous movement by the treacherous leaders of the N.A.A.C.P., the servile preachers of the Chattanooga Interdenominational Ministers Alliance; the tool of the steel bosses, Mr. Vann of the Pittsburgh *Courier*; the bankrupt national reformist leaders of the Garvey movement and other petty beneficiaries of the imperialist system under which the Negro masses are robbed and oppressed. These are seeking to strangle the thunderous cry rising from millions of workers throughout the land, THEY SHALL NOT DIE!

These traitors have joined with the southern boss lynchers in their attacks on the defense of the nine boys. With the most disgusting hypocrisy they are attempting to trick the Negro masses into the belief that they are defending the boys, just as they attempted, unsuccessfully to trick the nine boys and their parents into repudiation of the I.L.D. and the mass movement which alone can save the boys, by its mass pressure on the southern courts in support of the legal defense marshaled by the I.L.D.

But that thunderous cry THEY SHALL NOT DIE continues to grow and spread throughout the width and breadth of the land,

and is even now being taken up by tens of thousands of workers in other countries, and by the liberated millions of the Soviet Union.

Together with the white masses who are rallying to the fight to save the nine youths, the Negro masses must give increasing emphasis to the demand THEY SHALL NOT DIE! Neither the attacks of the bosses nor the treacherous activities of the Negro reformists must be permitted to prevent the growth of the mass movement to save these boys. All resistance must be swept out of the way, and with the resistance the traitors as well.

The task of saving the nine Negro boys is not only the job of the I.L.D. and the L.S.N.R. and the hundreds of organizations supporting the united front defense campaign, but the job of every individual white and Negro worker and poor farmer. Raise the question of defense in your shops, in your neighborhoods! Build Block committees of 3 or 5 or 10 or more! Raise the questions of support for the defense in your organization, in your lodges, in the churches! See that your organization participates in every protest parade, in every demonstration, in every united front conference called by the I.L.D. and L.S.N.R. for the purpose of mobilizing the masses and voicing our protest against this outrage. Smash the resistance of the Uncle Tom leaders to the fight to save these boys! Expose their open cooperation with the Southern boss lynchers! See that your organization gives financial support to the International Labor Defense which is the only organization defending these boys in the boss court. Organize your own block committees, as well, and collect funds and rush them in to the International Labor Defense, 80 East 11ᵗʰ Street, Room 430, New York City.

Only a gigantic mass movement, only the grim resolve of the masses THEY SHALL NOT DIE can save these boys and smash the murderous frame-up against them.

Records of the International Labor Defense, Schomburg Center for Research in Black Culture, New York Public Library

"No Race Hatred in Worker's Russia"

Labor Defender

July 1931

William L. Patterson

Never in the history of the struggles of the Negro masses of America was it so important that they take full stock of their miserable position.

To the mob violence, lynch terror, discrimination and segregation which is every day a part of their lives has been added all of the burdens of this period of hard times—unemployment, wage cuts, speed-up on the job and starvation. Where is the solution? Have oppressed nations no escape from oppression? To these questions the Russian Revolution with its slogan of the right of self-determination to oppressed minorities gives an adequate answer.

Nineteen hundred and fourteen saw the beginning of a world war supposedly for the liberation of "small nations", for the right of national minorities to have a voice in their own government. Of the millions of soldiers on the fighting front more than two-thirds came from national groups which were politically and economically exploited and oppressed by the great nations.

But the end of the war was for the submerged peoples characterized in all cases save one by the transfer of masters. Newly created European states came into being only as pawns of the great powers in the struggles for markets and sources of raw material. Only in Eastern Europe did freedom come to any oppressed nations and there when the workers and farmers took the government in their own hands.

More than fifty different oppressed national groups whose position was like that of the 13,000,000 Negroes in the U.S.A. paid tribute to the Czar. Free cultural life was denied these people. They lived only to advance the glory of "great Russia." But those who steered the reins of struggle for a government of workers and farmers believed that only the voluntary cooperation of peoples, who controlled their own political and cultural life could be free from the blood feuds, national hatreds, programs, prejudices and discriminations which marked the pathway of national minorities under the czar.

To these minority groups the right of self-determination was extended by the new Workers' and Peasants' Government. There were no reservations. This right included the right of complete separation. Latvia, Lithuania, Finland and several other states elected under the influence of former privileged classes to break away and did. Yet the masses in these countries became enslaved by their own ruling classes who were but the tools of Western imperialism.

The freedom of those who elected to remain part of the Soviet Union was complete. They secured political and cultural self-rule. The peasants were freed from age-old slavery to the soil and to the cities. Loans came from the state. Machines began to take the place of wooden agricultural implements. The workers and peasants in their own Soviets became their own masters. Women were freed from their enslavement to men and household drudgery for the first time in the history of the world. The native language came back to the schools.

The cultural backwardness of these peoples, forced upon them by the ruling class of the oppressor nation, was the basis for the theory of their inferiority. The wiping out of that backwardness and the explosion of the inferiority idea is a product of workers' and peasants' self-rule.

The solution of the question of oppressed nationalities is of the utmost importance to the millions of Negroes in the Southern states, the millions of Mexicans in the Southwest, and the other national groups oppressed by American imperialism.

These oppressed millions must give the utmost attention to passing events. History has put on the order of the day the solution of their problem.

Fond 515, Files of the Communist Party of the United States in the Comintern Archives

The Negro Worker

July 1931

Increase and Spread the Scottsboro Defense.

The storm of international protest against the planned execution of 8 young Negro workers on a frame-up charge, at Scottsboro, Alabama, that has arisen throughout the world and grows in volume, has shocked the bourgeoisie. ONLY MIGHTY MASS PROTEST OF THE INTERNATIONAL PROLETARIAT CAN STOP THE EXECUTION OF THE 8 BLACK PROLETARIANS!

Mass demonstrations and meetings of workers of all races as well as stormy scenes before American consulates have been held throughout Europe and America, and in South Africa and Latin America, protesting indignantly against the frame-up of their class brothers and demanding their release. NOTHING LIKE THIS HAS EVER HAPPENED BEFORE! The bourgeoisie has been astounded at this wonderful demonstration of international solidarity—AT THE SPECTACLE OF WORKERS OF ALL THE RACES RAISING THEIR FISTS IN DEFENSE OF 8 NEGRO PROLETARIANS.

At Berlin workers, under the leadership of the Communist Party and the International Labor Defense made mighty demonstrations before the American consulate.

At Paris a demonstration before the American consulate was broken up by the police.

In South Africa native and poor white workers themselves ground down under the heel of Boer and British imperialism raised their protest.

At Hamburg and extending into the country districts over 5 huge mass meetings and demonstrations have been held; comrade Andre, the well known leader of the Red Front Fighters, and others have spoken. Altogether over 20,000 workers have taken part, and the wave of protest has been great.

On July 9th a great mass meeting was held at the International Seamen's Club at Hamburg in which African seamen took part. Representatives of the International Labor Defense and the International Trade Union Committee of Negro Workers spoke on the history of the case and its class significance. The mass of workers expressed their indignation by protest resolutions denouncing the frame-up of these boys by the American capitalists and demanding their immediate release. On the same day a demonstration was held at the American consulate.

At Dresden and Cologne, Germany, windows of the American consulates were broken in and the workers hurled bottles into the windows containing messages: Stop the Lynching! Hands off the 8 Negro Workers! In these and many other towns of Germany the workers have demonstrated under the leadership of the Communist Party and the Labor Defense.

At Geneva, Switzerland, on the occasion of the holding of the International Conference on African Children, the frame-up was denounced before this body by the representative of the League Against Imperialism. On the following day a protest meeting was held in Geneva at which a representative of the International Trade Union Committee of Negro workers spoke. Under the Leadership of the Swiss Section of the International Labor Defense, workers demonstrated before the American consulate. They paraded through the streets despite the police order against it and then held their meeting before the Consulate. The police tried to break up the meeting but the workers fought back, several were arrested. The walls of the American consulate building were painted with Big Red letters: *Down With Lynch Rule in U.S.A.! Stop the Murder of the 8 Negro Boys!*

Workers in many other countries in England, Cuba, etc., have joined in the International protest. In Moscow and Leningrad and many other cities and factories throughout Russia mighty mass demonstrations arose in indignant protestation against this most brutal frame-up of 8 children by American capitalism.

Comrades, this international spirit of solidarity is the only kind of language that the bourgeoisie will heed. This mass movement bringing about the solidarity of workers throughout the world, will bring so much pressure upon the bloody thirsty capitalist bosses of the U.S.A. that they will be forced to release our class brothers.

Telegrams and cables have poured in upon the Governor of Alabama from over the world. A cable of protest was received from a group of scientists with the name of Albert Einstein, the famous German scientist at the top. At Leningrad there was a great protest of the toiling cultural and scientific workers, engineers, technicians, educational and art workers.

This has been a mighty demonstration of world sympathy and international solidarity.

But comrades and fellow workers, the boys are still in the clutches of the fiendish boss class. Only an appeal to a higher court has delayed the case so far. There is nothing but capitalist "justice" in these courts. This means that the boys will be executed unless we raise a mightier international protest for their actual release.

The International Trade Union Committee of Negro Workers calls upon the international proletariat to increase its vigilance, to increase its protests. Demonstrate before American consulates! Let the bosses feel the mighty fist of the international proletariat!

To the workers of Alabama both white and black, organize Self-Defense Corps composed of both white and black workers. Defend your right to assembly! Defend your meetings! Demonstrate for the release of the boys! You are fighting for bread and life. The bosses are trying to hide from you unemployment and starvation. They are trying to divide you and thereby destroy your movement.

Down with white terror and lynching. Death to Lynchers!

Long live International solidarity!

Fond 515, Files of the Communist Party of the United States in the Comintern Archives

Negro Bureau of the Comintern.

B. D. Amis Speech at the 13th Plenum, CPUSA

September, 1931

In the 20 minutes I have I want to deal with one point. And that is because the Party today is engaged in such a struggle that it is necessary that we must have the fullest clarification relative to the struggles we are conducting for Negro rights in order that this tremendous influence we have among the Negro masses may be turned into organizational results. No one will deny the fact that the Party has an overwhelming amount of influence among the Negro masses. This is best shown in their participation in the various demonstrations that the Party, the TUUL have held, also in the hunger marches and in the numerous other campaigns the Party has conducted. On August 1st, in the Party demonstrations against the war danger, here we can see a great upward trend in the number of participants of Negroes in the hundreds of demonstrations. For instance, in places like in the North, in Minnesota, etc., we see that these workers are not so very familiar with our systematic and energetic fight against the war danger, for the protection of the Soviet Union, but because of the correct approach of the Party, we were able to draw out large numbers to demonstrate. This influence the Party has, has been the result of the Party beginning to conduct gigantic struggles in the fight for Negro rights. We have recorded positive achievements since the last Plenum. For instance, the Yokinen trial in New York which laid the very foundation for the absolute turn in our work in the Negro field.

The next large struggle was the developing of a large mass movement around the Scottsboro campaign and here, comrades, I want to dwell for quite a few moments, for the reason that in the Scottsboro campaign we have for the first time in the Party a gigantic struggle which has two aspects in the struggle for Negro rights, the national questions and the class question.

Because of the united front policy we have carried on, we were able to mobilize hundreds of thousands of Negroes to participate in the building up of a mass defense movement in the Scottsboro campaign. However, because of the fact that we were able to win the mothers of all the boys to support us in this campaign, because we were able to mobilize thousands of Negro workers to help us build up this movement, we did not exploit these opportunities to the fullest extent.

The comrades did not understand the peculiar role of the Negro workers. For instance, when we decided to bring every mother to the North to conduct an energetic campaign in order to mobilize thousands of Negro workers to protest against the frameup, the comrades were not conscious of the necessity to pay special attention to the care of these mothers. I want to state that I believe that our comrades in Philadelphia do not receive our CC directives or they don't read them. We were very careful when we knew we had in our hands a weapon which could become the sharpest instrument with which we could break down the illusions of the white liberals and petty-bourgeois reformist Negroes by utilizing these mothers to help build up this mass movement. In every district, however, we see a looseness and a most criminal carelessness in the handling of the mothers.

In Philadelphia, we sent Mrs. Powell, the mother of the one of the boys. What did they do? We stated in our directive that these mothers must be placed with responsible Party comrades who should have the task of always and constantly guiding and watching over them. Mrs. Powell, however, was placed with the rankest sort of white chauvinist who put her to work washing dishes, scrubbing floors, washing dyties, etc.

Now, comrades, however, after the Philadelphia comrades had this deplorable situation drawn to their attention, some steps were made to correct this. But after Mrs. Powell was brought here to New York, where we take pride in having certain facilities to make these mothers more comfortable and help develop them, even here our comrades fell down on the job, placing her in an isolated home or rather a meeting hall in the most foul air and dirty quarters.

This shows what, comrades? First of all, that the comrades were not aware of the hazardous situation they placed us in. If our enemies would have found out that we handled the mothers like we did, what would have been the result? Take it the other way. If we knew these mothers were handled like this by the NAACP, would we not jump at their throats in meetings, conferences, etc.? Our comrades do not recognize that in dealing with the question, we have a special question and we cannot treat this question like we treat the ordinary question and like we treat the white workers. From now on, the comrades must recognize that fact that in dealing with the Negro question they have a special task. And that is our task to show the Negro workers—yes, we are going to fight for their rights and to show them we are going to carry on an energetic campaign in order to prove that the things we put in writing will be carried out in practice. In the Camp Hill case, it was a result of our Scottsboro campaign, that the Negro peasants in Alabama were willing to carry on a campaign linking this case up with the Scottsboro case and other campaigns we were carrying on.

We noticed a decided lagging in this campaign. However, there was another campaign which proved a sort of a boomerang. The Chicago massacre and here we find a rise in the curve. The struggles that the comrades in Chicago conducted gave a little bit more of an impetus to the Scottsboro and the Camp Hill campaign.

Now as to some of the mistakes of the Scottsboro campaign. First I think we have to charge ourselves with making these mistakes and one of the crassest in my opinion in this campaign was when we started out to build block and neighborhood committees. Not that we should not have built them. This is the most effective way in which we could reach the masses by our united front from below, but we began to build block committees and neighborhood committees in certain districts and restricted and narrowed the base only to the issue of struggle to save the nine boys. This is not the correct policy. The policy should have been, and we did change afterwards, that the workers drawn into the block and neighborhood committees should not only be drawn into the struggle to save the nine Scottsboro boys but that we should raise the level of their struggles, draw them into further political campaigns that we would develop their class-consciousness and develop their mood for struggle against all forms of oppression and exploitation.

Another mistake and this was noticeable in almost every district. The comrades in trying to build united front movements from below followed in the tail of the Negro misleaders such [as the] NAACP and churches, going there and appealing to the "fair-play" of these misleaders and for them to appeal to "their" masses in the campaign. We would have built up mere genuine mass movement if we had absolutely ignored these misleaders and went about building the block and neighborhood commit- tees and we would have drawn thousands more into the struggle than we did. Another mistake was the open arms with which we accepted one of the worst types of reactionary misleaders of the Negro masses, when Pickens wrote the International Labor Defense and sent them a few dollars endorsing the campaign, we came out with great big headlines welcoming Pickens into the struggle, stating that he had joined the struggle without exposing his reactionary role and without telling the masses that his action was caused not by his sincerity but by the mass pressure forcing him to take such a step. This we failed to do and this is a bad mis- take. Closely connected with this was another serious mistake which I made myself and I want to take full responsibility for this. And this is the editorial which appeared in the Liberator last week where we also gave the crassest manifestation of Right wing opportunism in appealing to the bourgeois press to more ener- getically take up the struggle for Negro rights. I will not go into the details of what was the content of the editorial but it is suffi- cient to state that the contents were of such character that there was tendency to create false illusions among the Negro masses that they could rely on their Negro reformist leaders, that they would begin to struggle for their rights. Also that we somehow expected these petty-bourgeois reactionary newspaper leaders to use the column of their press to expose the white terror and oppression and exploitation of the Negro masses. Another dan- ger is that we did not link up the struggle of the Negro masses with the struggle of the white workers. And this brought into more sharp expression that in this appeal we absolutely distorted the role of the Liberator. And after we get through reading this editorial one would think that the Negro press will become an effective force to mobilize the Negro masses for struggle. Then there is no room for the Liberator?

Such mistakes hinder and hamper our struggle in mobilizing masses of Negro workers to participate in joint struggle with the white workers and it is necessary at this time that whatever we put into the press, our policies must be clear-cut decisive and correct.

Now comrades, in regard to the struggle today in the Negro field, some comrades have raised the question, because of these partial successes (and I want to state that in Chicago where they have had partial success that they are now on the brink of the danger point). Here is a tremendous amount of influence built up among the Negro workers in the South side of Chicago and now we have an opportunity to show that we as a Communist Party, as a Bolshevik Party can take this influence among the thousands of Negro workers and turn it into organizational gains and build our Party, that we can build our revolutionary unions, that we can build our LSNR, that we can build our Liberator into a mass organ. Unless we are able to realize some organizational results from this mass influence that we have in Chicago we will have to acknowledge that we are absolutely very weak, and the campaign will almost amount to nought. Some of the comrades realize the successes of these struggles of the share croppers in Alabama, because of the struggles in Chicago and Scottsboro, because of the militancy of the Negro workers in Birmingham in fighting police terror the comrades say they think it is time to raise a new perspective—whether we are in an insurrectionary period or not. We must have a new perspective.

We are not ready now to raise the question of a new perspective, neither are the Negro masses in a period of insurrection. Our task is to develop further the struggles of the Negro workers, economic struggles, political struggles, struggles for their day to day needs. Another task is to link up the struggles of the Negro masses with the struggles of the white proletariat. If we concern ourselves with these major tasks and develop the fighting political consciousness the next stage of their struggles will come and we will not have to worry about looking for it. To develop the struggles against the evictions, for immediate unemployment relief, against high rents, discrimination, terror and persecution, etc. is still our perspective for the present time, as well as developing joint struggles of the black and white workers.

Records of the International Labor Defense, Schomburg Center for Research in Black Culture, New York Public Library

"Scottsboro—And the Nice People"

Labor Defender

August 1931

Eugene Gordon

The following is taken from an article written by Eugene Gordon, a brilliant young Negro writer and contributor to many American magazines. Mr. Gordon, indignant at the attempt of the National Association for the Advancement of Colored People to split the united front being built by the I.L.D. to save the boys, exposes the N.A.A.C.P. in its true role—terming it the "Nice Association for the Advancement of Certain People." This article also portrays William Pickens, field secretary of the N.A.A.C.P. in his true light.

Now that the N.A.A.C.P. has discovered that there is a "Scottsboro case," the black and white workers of the country may get ready for some amusing moments. They may even prepare for some good belly laughs, if they can find the courage to laugh in the face of starvation, evictions and persecutions in general. But the N.A.A.C.P. and its cohorts are laughing, and if *they* can do it, why shouldn't the workers laugh, too? Of course, the members of the Nice Association are laughing at the Scottsboro case: really, it is the funniest thing they have ever heard of. Let Mr. William Pickens, the Association's field secretary, tell you the story, if you don't believe it's funny.

The Boston branch of the Nice Association held a meeting the other night, having chosen for its rendezvous what the daily papers referred to the next day as "the fashionable Mount Vernon Congregational Church at Massachusetts Avenue and Beacon Street." The Mount Vernon Congregational Church is at least a mile and a half away from the nearest Negro church in the South End.

The pastor of the Church, the Rev. Mr. Sidney Lovett, spoke telling how glad he was to open his doors in behalf of justice. We are all children of the same Father, you know, and "we are coming to realize that God is no respecter of persons." He said also that "obedience to law is liberty," and his audience of High Colored Society clapped its manicured hands with cultivated studiedness. Advising his hearers not to judge Alabama and the South "too harshly," because "we have been known to have lynching even in the North," the Rev. Mr. Lovett walked sanctimoniously to the rear of the church and sat down.

Then came Mr. William Pickens, and the audience forgot where it was and guffawed. Pickens has that effect on one, it seems. He appeared to like it. Launching immediately into an account of his visit at Scottsboro, he described the case with all the noted Pickensian humor. The audience was now in the festive frame of mind. Those who had sat slumped in their seats, evidently expecting to hear sordid details of an unpleasant story, perked up and smacked their lips. It was as if having been bored by tenth-rate stunts at a vaudeville show, their favorite comedian had suddenly come up on stage. The chief laughing point of the speaker's talk was his description of the difficulties the nine boys would have encountered trying to rape two white prostitutes atop a sand-pile on a flat car. Every time he alluded to that point the audience forgot its surroundings, its culture, its apings, and laughed aloud. It was a great show.

The Rev. Samuel Weems, of the North Cambridge Congregational Church, the only Negro minister in Greater Boston who has shown himself to be one of the workers, leading in the fight constantly night after night and Sunday after Sunday, rose and demanded to be heard. The fashionable audience was dumbfounded. Mr. Wilson stood poised like a frightened gray squirrel. The Rev. Mr. Sidney Lovett stood looking perplexedly around in the rear of the church. A sergeant of police and two patrolmen swaggered down the aisle looking menacingly into the pews. Shouts rose all over the house: "We demand to be heard!" "We demand that the audience be told the truth about the Scottsboro frame-up!" "We demand the right to ask questions!"

In the vestry Mr. Wilson apologized for this unseemly conduct, addressing Mr. Lovett. The crowd flowed around the walls and waited for something to happen. Mr. Wilson backed against the wall and flanked by two brutish policemen, said that Mr. Pickens would be glad to answer any question seeking information about the case.

"Mr. Pickens," someone shouted, "is it not true that at the beginning of the Scottsboro case you said you did not know why the N.A.A.C.P. was not doing anything, and is it not true that you contributed to the I.L.D. to help defend these boys? Why are you attacking the I.L.D. now, Mr. Pickens?" Stumped for a moment, the noted N.A.A.C.P. end man cleared his throat and said: "Yes, I did say that, not knowing that the N.A.A.C.P. was silently working on the case while I was away out there in Oklahoma. And as for my helping, I would help the devil if I thought he would save these boys."

"I'll tell you a little story," he offered. But one of the workers shouted, "We're here to hear you answer questions, not tell little stories." This uppercut made Dean Pickens mad, and he shouted that he would answer questions in any way he saw fit. He started again. Someone in the rear called him to order. The ex-attorney-general, pale as his handkerchief, suggested to Mr. Wilson that the church had been let to them only until ten, and since it was now ten minutes after, they should adjourn. Mr. Wilson grasped at this straw and declared the meeting adjourned.

A Call to Millions

Daily Worker
January 21, 1932.

Appeal of the Scottsboro Mothers

To the working class mothers of the world:

We are the mothers of the nine Scottsboro Negro boys who have been sentenced to die on the electric chair. The world knows our poor boys is innocent. We appeal to all working class mothers to help us save our boys from being killed.

It might have happened to any working class mother's boy. We've been starving all our lives and forced to live from hand to mouth, working for as low as $2.50 a week down here in the South and our boys wanted to go out and find work to help us out. We didn't want to let them go because they are almost only babies. One of them is thirteen years old, and two are only fourteen. The oldest ain't over twenty.

And now here they is in Kilby prison waiting for the electric chair. For something they ain't never done. They was put in jail at Scottsboro on frame-up. Everybody knows now they never did commit that rape the boss-men down here charge them with. They was framed up only because they are working class boys, and because they are Negroes. That is all. Nothing else. They been saved from the electric chair so far by the working class led by the League of Struggle for Negro Rights and the International Labor Defense. We thought we had no friends but when we went to some of them mass meeting we saw the working class to know the white boss men down here mean to send our poor boys to the chair. That's why we make this appeal for bigger meetings, more help to the League of Struggle for Negro Rights and the International Labor Defense.

The NAACP try to sell-out on us. But we knew they were our enemies. We stopped them in time. They works in hand with the white men down here.

Our boys was framed up in the trial at Scottsboro. There was a lynching mob outside the door hollering for our boys to die.

Working class mothers—these boys might a been your boys. It makes no difference nowadays whether the skin's white or black. The boss man's framing up trouble for all workers. Only in the South here it's especially the worker with the black skin who gets it worse.

We calls on you to help us save our boys. They done nothing your boys might not have done. They looked for jobs. That's all. We was starving and they looked for jobs. Help the International Labor Defense and the League of Struggle for Negro Rights to raise bigger meetings and show the boss men the working class won't let our boys die for nothing. Help us get them free! They only looked for jobs.

(Signed)
Bernice Morris
Viola Montgomery
Ada Wright
Janie Patterson
Josephine Powell

Mamie Williams
Ida Norris

Records of the International Labor Defense, Schomburg Center for Research in Black Culture, New York Public Library

"The NAACP—Assistant Hangman"

Labor Defender

January 1932.

Harry Haywood,

What has prevented the execution of the Scottsboro boys? Why were they not burned on schedule on June 10, 1930?

There is only one answer: because the workers of the world roared their protest. Because the International Labor Defense, the League of Struggle for Negro Rights, and every working-class group throughout the world turned upon the lynchers the glaring spotlight of exposure. Squirming in this fierce light, they were forced to stop their bloody work.

What did this spotlight reveal? It revealed in all of its hideous nakedness the system of serfdom and robbery of the Negro masses. It revealed the nature of boss-class justice in the courts. It revealed how these courts are the instruments of the slave-drivers and lynchers for the purpose of maintaining the whole system of super-exploitation of the Negro masses.

The lynchers knew that this exposure of their system would weaken the authority of their courts. They feared that it would awaken the Negro masses to a deeper sense of the injustice of the system, and stimulate among these masses a desire to struggle against their oppressors. This would make their rule more difficult.

But all of those who wished to save the nine Scottsboro boys, all the workers who hated the lynchers and their system, were glad of this spotlight. For they knew that it was this alone that saved the innocent boys from the electric chair.

But the enemies of the boys hated the roar of the workers' voices. All those who wished to see the boys die, all who feared to disturb the slavery and terror of boss rule, banded together and shouted: "Take away the spotlight! Let the voices of the workers be stilled! Do not disturb the lynchers at their work. Do not anger the slave-drivers!"

One of the loudest voices in this pack was the voice of the N.A.A.C.P. It screamed with anger! At the lynchers? No! It screamed at those who mercilessly held the spotlight upon the lynchers.

The N.A.A.C.P. entered the case to defend the lynchers, and their system, and not the intended victims of the lynching. They defended the court which sentenced them and did not defend the victims. They hired the lawyer Roddy, who betrayed the nine Negro boys in the trial, and they did not defend the victims of Roddy's treachery. The N.A.A.C.P. protested against calling the prosecution and trial of nine innocent boys an outrage, and refused to defend the victims of this outrage. They were concerned with maintaining the confidence of the American masses in the courts that perpetrate legal lynchings like that against the nine Scottsboro boys, but they were not concerned with saving these intended victims from the outrage of the court. They raised the cry of the "red menace" even more loud than the lynchers, thus putting weapons into the hands of the slave-drivers and lynchers.

Why?

Because the official leadership of the N.A.A.C.P. does not represent the interests of the Negro toilers. It represents that class among the Negroes which has stake in the system of exploitation and segregations—Negro bourgeoisie. The ruling white imperialists which demand the lion share of the profits coming from the special exploitation of the Negro toilers, in the industries, and on the plantations, hands on [to] the Negro bourgeoisie the remaining juicy crumbs of exorbitant profits to be gained from the perpetuation of the Negro ghettoes. This Negro class which includes the real estate brokers, the owners of insurance companies, the bankers, and other such commercial groups, also a section of the most influential Negro professionals are interested in maintaining the Negro ghettoes as the basis of their existence.

In this manner the white ruling class fosters a buffer class between itself and the Negro masses, an ally which it uses to throttle the growing militancy of the Negro toilers against their brutal oppression. It is precisely this community of interests which is the basis of the "holy alliance" between the white imperialist masters and their Negro reformist lackeys against the Negro masses. These masses must not be blinded by the phrases of these reformists who wage slum battles against the white ruling class in their quarrel for larger share of the profits.

Therefore the growing unity of Negro and white workers, as in the fight against the Scottsboro frame-up by attacking the whole system of segregation and exploitation threatens the very existence of this parasitic Negro bourgeoisie—and threatens the leadership of its chief representative, the N.A.A.C.P. (the Whites, Pickens, Du Bois, etc.) professional racketeers battening on the misery of the Negro masses. It is apparent from the above facts that the role of the N.A.A.C.P. in the Scottsboro case, stands exposed as that of assistant hangman to the bosses. Therefore the struggle of the workers for the freedom of legal and otherwise must have as one of its chief centers of attack, the N.A.A.C.P. and the whole tribe of Negro reformists.

Fond 515, Files of the Communist Party of the United States in the Comintern Archives

Executive Committee of International Red Aid

Executive of the International Trade Union Committee of Negro Workers

April 1932

To the Toilers of All Countries!

The American imperialists have all preparations made for a new outrage against the working class. The burning to death by electrocution, of the eight Negro boys at Scottsboro remains fixed for April 6th.

The American bourgeoisie, faced on the one hand with the greatest economic crisis in its history and on the other hand with the increasing revolutionary militancy of the white and Negro toilers, is desperately trying to smash their united front in their common struggle against unemployment, wage cuts, rationalization, bourgeois class justice and white terror. The chief victims are the brutally oppressed and exploited Negro toiling masses. This is why a new wave of lynchings is sweeping over the United States.

This terror is not enough to satisfy the Negro-hating landlords and cotton-mill barons of the South. They are more than ever determined to burn to death these eight Negro boys, the youngest of whom is only 13 years old and the oldest, only 20 years. The death sentence still hangs over these boys, the sons of workers and tenant-farmers, while the representatives of the bourgeoisie—the State Supreme Court—"consider" the appeal.

The object of this execution, as of the rising class terror all over the United States, is to strike fear into the hearts of the toiling masses, both white and black; to crush out their organized protest against the active participation of American capitalism in the imperialist war already started in the Far East and in the preparation for military intervention against the Soviet Union.

These continued outrages against the toiling masses and the Negroes in the United States have resulted in a world-wide wave of indignant protests and burning condemnation among the workers of America itself and those of every other country. In the face of the open hostility and attacks of the ultra-reactionary American Federation of Labor, the social-fascists, the Negro reformist National Association for the Advancement of Colored People and the Universal Negro Improvement Association (Garvey) which are objectively supporting this frame-up, the workers of the whole world have already raised their protest under the leadership of the International Red Aid, the International Trade Union Committee of Negro Workers and other revolutionary organizations.

The workers cannot put trust in the "justice" of the bourgeois courts. We have not forgotten the Mooney-Billings case, the Sacco-Vanzetti execution, the Harlan frame-ups! It is only the mass protest actions of the working class throughout the world that can restrain the labor hating capitalists and landlords of the state of Alabama from carrying out their murder programme.

Mass Action and International Solidarity Must Save Them!

Toilers in all countries!

Demand the immediate, unconditional release of the Scottsboro Negro boys, including the boy sentenced to life imprisonment!

Down with the lynching of Negro workers in America!

For the united front of the Negro and white workers of the United States against the class terror of the bourgeoisie and their social-fascist and national-reformist agents! Long live the international solidarity of the toilers of all races and nationalities.

Records of the International Labor Defense, Schomburg Center for Research in Black Culture, New York Public Library

"Scottsboro Before the World"

Labor Defender

April 1932.

James W. Ford,

At the opening of the Hamburg Conference of Negro Workers a widespread wave of terror was being carried on against the Negro toilers in the United States. New waves of terror are now sharpening against the whole working class of the United States.

The Hamburg Conference of Negro Workers correctly estimated the growing resistance of the Negro toilers not only in the United States but thruout the Negro world. The Negro toilers everywhere were staggering under burdens placed on their shoulders by the capitalist imperialists. There was not a Negro colony nor any section of the United States where the effects of the economic crisis were not causing untold misery to the masses of Negro toilers.

In South Africa, Madagascar, Kenya Colony, Gambia, Nigeria, the French and Belgian Congo, Guadaloupe, Honduras, San Domingo, Haiti, the Negro masses have taken up arms in the struggle against the terrible conditions placed upon their shoulders. Almost immediately, a wave of imperialist terror was started in an attempt to stifle the resistance of the Negro toilers. Here is what is carried on in—Black Africa and the Negro Movement the destruction of native villages in the Sudan and Central Africa by the French imperialists because the natives refuse to pay taxes, the same in Sierra Leone by the British imperialists who at the same time killed many native peasants, also in the Belgian Congo where only recently a revolt of the natives has been suppressed by the ruthless slaughter of natives; suppression of the harbor workers strike in Dahomey, suppressions in Madagascar—jail hard labor for non-payment of taxes; the shooting down of native women in Nigeria by the British imperialists; suppression of the movement of the natives in East Africa, and brutal murdering of native workers in South Africa on Dingaan's Day, slugging and brutality on May 1st when the workers stormed the houses of the rich demanding work and relief from unemployment; the reign of murderous lynch law in the U.S.A., the frame-up and sentencing of eight Negro boys in Alabama to be electrocuted; the suppression of the workers and peasants movement in the West Indies by U.S. marines.

Subjections, Plans for War

All of this is proof that the capitalists and their native lackeys are not only trying to smash the struggles of the colonial masses for freedom, but are also trying to safeguard themselves in case of war, by having the colonial masses and oppressed races completely subjugated.

New exceptional laws, the increased taking of the land of the natives, the intensified terroristic measures of the white slaveholders, the wave of terror, lynchings and persecutions in the U.S.A., have been unable to stop the rising tide of the Negro's struggle for emancipation from colonial imperialism, from brutal exploitation and oppression in the United States. *New and tremendous reserves of Negro masses are swung into the class struggle.*

Herein lies the significance and importance of the resistance of the Negro toilers on an *international scale*. Herein lies the significance of the Scottsboro case to the international working class and why workers in every country thruout the world, set up a storm of international protest.

Mass Demonstrations Thruout World

Mass demonstrations, meetings and conferences were held thruout the world. The International Trade Union Committee of Negro Workers, at Hamburg, was able to cooperate with workers in Europe. We received protests from workers in colonial countries. As far away as Australia, New Zealand and Japan, resolutions of solidarity and protest came in to us.

In Hamburg special meetings were held with African seamen where resolutions in protest against the Scottsboro frame-up and the persecution of Negroes generally were drawn up, discussed in detail and adopted.

International Seamen Join Fight

In some cases these meetings were held on board ships. The African comrades expressed great indignation at the treatment of their brothers in the U.S.A. They related their experiences in Africa, they told of the unspeakable butchery of African toilers by the imperialists in Africa.

On July 9th, 1931, a great interracial protest meeting of seamen was held at the International Seaman's Club at Hamburg. Many African seamen attended this meeting. German seamen and workers expressed great indignation at the treatment of their Negro brother workers.

German Workers Protest

German workers held demonstrations before the American Consulate at Hamburg, demanding the release of the Scottsboro boys.

In Berlin, Dresden, Cologne and other German cities, mass meetings of protest were held. In some cases, bottles were hurled thru windows of American consulates, containing messages which demanded the release of the Scottsboro boys.

Africa, India, China

In South Africa, protest meetings were held in defense of the Scottsboro boys. Resolutions were adopted in meetings of native and white workers. In Cuba and Latin and Central America, protest meetings have been held. From Chinese and Indian workers protests poured in.

In Soviet Russia, nation-wide mighty protests of workers and peasants against this brutal attack on the Negro workers in the U.S.A. was exposed.

In Moscow, Leningrad and other large industrial centers, mighty mass meetings were held. Cultural and scientific workers also took part in these demonstrations and protests.

Role of Reformists

On the occasion of the holding of the World Congress of the Second "Socialist" International in Vienna in July 1931, this writer spoke at several meetings in Austria exposing the role of the Second International in helping the imperialists exploit and oppress colonial toilers. He especially emphasized how the MacDonald "socialist" Labor Government supported slavery and brutality in Africa, how the French socialists support the bloody action of French imperialism in the French African colonies, how the Belgian socialists support bloody terror in the Belgian Congo and finally the attitude of socialists in the U.S.A. to lynchings of Negroes and the Scottsboro frame-up.

Hillquit of the U.S.A. was American delegate to the Congress of the Second International. He was feted in Vienna, while this writer was arrested, held in jail three days and deported from

Austria as an undesirable alien for his activities in behalf of oppressed people and the Scottsboro boys. Money was taken from his pockets by the Socialist Austrian administration to defray expenses of two police escorts to the Austrian border.

The Negro reformists and organizations, such as the National Association for the Advancement of Colored People in the U.S.A. have said that the International protest prejudiced the case of the Scottsboro boys. This shows not only how low they stoop to lick-splitting, but how they actually help capitalist bosses execute the boys.

Only international proletarian protest and organization stayed so far the execution of the Scottsboro boys!

In order to release the boys, the fight must be increased tenfold. *The international proletariat must raise its fist.*

Organize the united front of the working class against terror, lynching, hunger and imperialist war in China and the attack on the Soviet Union!

Records of the International Labor Defense, Schomburg Center for Research in Black Culture, New York Public Library

"A Call to Millions"

Labor Defender

June 1932.

Eugene Gordon [*On the eve of the bosses planned execution of the Scottsboro boys, June 24. Eugene Gordon was a well known Negro writer.*]

Fellow workers, the challenge has been thrown into our teeth by the bloodthirsty attorney general of Alabama. The face of the working class of the world has been slapped and spit upon by the arrogant member of the Alabama ruling class. The working class of the United States and of the world has been defied; its protests have been ignored, its petitions have been sneered [at] as the cries of horror at the threatened killing of nine boys on June 24th, as if they were nine hogs or steers chanting for the blood of workers. The attorney general of Alabama has sworn that the nine

Scottsboro victims will be burned to death as soon as their latest appeal has been denied. He takes the denial of this appeal as an assured fact. You see, he knows the working of ruling class justice. But he reckons without his host. He gloats and slobbers at his glee at seeing workers burned to death like waste, like rubbish, like so many sacrificial beasts. He gloats and slobbers because these boys are workers, and he defies the working class because these boys are black workers. He thinks of and longs for the time when black men and women were the property of those who today scorn them because they struggle against the barbarous oppression of their former owners. He would make an example of these working class boys for the black workers of the world to heed.

Fellow workers of America, shall we let this thing be done? Is there a white worker within the United States who feels himself secure so long as any worker, white or black, is murdered as an example to teach you your place? For it is an attempt to teach you and me our place. The attorney general hopes that no power on earth can halt him in carrying out the ruling class will to burn these boys. At the same time he knows [that if] the masses raised their clenched hands in one giant fist they can force him to release the 9 Negro boys. He is hiding behind the forces of the ruling-class law but he shivers in dread of the masses. His boast is a lie; his arrogance is a flimsy cloak to hide the yellow stripes along his spine.

Fellow workers, let us justify his fear. It is in our power to save those boys. It is mass protest that the ruling class dreads and fears. It is the mass shouts of anger that make them cringe. It is mass contempt for the their ruling-class arrogance that turns that arrogance into whimpers.

Let us demonstrate our determination to save our working-class comrades.

They must be released.

They must not die!

We only can release them. It is our job as workers. It is a task *that must be done!*

Records of the International Labor Defense, Schomburg Center for Research in Black Culture, New York Public Library

"Scottsboro and Beyond."

Labor Defender

June 1932.

Harry Haywood

In the midst of the intense, world-wide fight for the freedom of the Scottsboro victims, it is well to get perspective view of the larger issue involved in the case. The Scottsboro frame-up is not an isolated instance of persecution; it is part and parcel of a huge, cold-blooded system of oppression and terrorization of millions of Negro toilers, a system that has been well nigh reduced to a science by the boss class that imposes it.

This boss terror against an oppressed National minority finds its most open and violent expression in lynching, an institution which is rooted deeply in the economic system which gives it birth and nourishes it. The present economic crisis, the growing capitalist offensive against the mounting struggle of the workers of all races reveals more clearly than ever before this economic class basis of Negro lynching. It can no longer be denied that lynching and lynch frame-ups are invariably the direct result of developing class struggles. Lynch Law is the threat facing the Negro workers who attempt or dare to struggle against wage cuts and evictions or for unemployment insurance, the Negro share cropper or farm laborer who protests against the virtual peonage imposed upon him by landlords and loan-sharks. These lynchings of recent occurrences, chosen at random, amply illustrate the class background of the infamous practice.

The murder of Ralph Gray at Camp Hill, Alabama, by a posse of sheriffs and landlords, for his activity in the organization of the Croppers Union.

The lynch frame up of Willie Peterson, disabled and unemployed Negro war veteran, avowedly as part of the reign of terror intended to suppress the forward movement toward organization

among the Negro and white workers and share croppers of
Alabama.

The murder of three Negro workers in Chicago and of two
in Cleveland shot down by policemen in connection with the
struggle against evictions.

Added to these instances are the wanton murders of individual Negro unemployed workers by sheriffs and police in every
part of the country for non-payment of rent. Recently a large
number of destitute workers suffering from cold and starvation
were shot down by company detectives in various towns for
picking up coal or fuel along railroad tracks.

Two tendencies are evident in this systematic persecution of
Negro workers. First, we find that more and more the boss class
with rope, faggot and gun, etc. with its newly perfected device of
"legal lynching" or lynching by "due process of (capitalist) law"
legal lynching is just as effective as string the victim up a tree, the
capitalists think. It is safer, less "scandalous," being covered by the
respectable cloak of capitalist "justice" and is invariably accompanied by the praise and thanks of such bootlicking, reformist
organizations as the National Association for the Advancement of
Colored People.

The Scottsboro case, the most outstanding example of legal
lynching contains all the typical elements of the damnable frame
up system, the trumped up charges and the lying testimony of
State witnesses, the speedy mockery of a trial in a carefully
whipped up atmosphere of lynch mania, the hand-picked jury
and prejudiced judge, denial of the most elemental rights to the
Negro victims who are doomed to death in advance, etc.

Other notable examples of the legal lynching system are the
cases of Euel Lee (Orphan Jones) in Maryland, Willie Brown in
Philadelphia, Willie Peterson in Birmingham, Jess Hollins in
Oklahoma and Bonny Lee Ross in Texas. In refusing to grant a
stay of execution to young Ross, who was railroaded to the electric chair, Governor Ross Sterling of Texas brazenly admitted the
role of lynching as a weapon in the boss campaign of suppression of the Negro masses in stating that "it may be that this man

is innocent, but it is some times necessary to burn a house in order to save a village."

Another dangerous trend in the present growth of boss inspired lynch mania is the passing from the stage [of] individual lynchings to armed terrorist attacks against whole communities by organized bands of fascist lynchers, Ku Kluxers, Black shirts, Legionnaires, etc. This tendency was apparent in the mass slaughter and disarming of Negroes in the Birmingham district of the time of the Willie Peterson frame up and in the ruthless terrorization of Negro comrades along the Eastern shore of Maryland during recent lynch fever, particularly in connection with the lynching of Matthew Williams in Salisbury, which was accompanied by a series of the most provocative acts against the Negro masses in that vicinity. In this instance, the body of the dying Williams was dragged through the streets of the Negro neighborhood, his fingers and toes were cut off and thrown on the porches of Negro houses and the lynchers shouted threats to whole Negro population.

The contemptible Ku Klux practice of "night riding" has been resumed in some parts of the south, as illustrated in the very recent incident at Greenfield, Tenn., where a band of cowardly fascists rode down on a Negro community during the night, hurling threats at the workers and burning several shacks.

The ruling class has [a] two-fold purpose in fostering this vicious campaign of terror against the Negro toilers (1) by whipping up lynch hysteria, it aims to divide the workers, and thus to weaken them. (2) it aims by this means to keep in terrorized subjection the Negro masses who constitute a great portion of the American working class.

Against this growing lynch terror, the American workers Negro and white must carry on a wide relentless struggle. It is absolutely essential for all workers to realize that the sharpening of the lynch terror is an integral factor in the general campaign of capitalist reaction against the toilers as a whole aimed particularly to strike at the growing unity of Negro and white workers.

Records of the International Labor Defense, Schomburg Center for Research in Black Culture, New York Public Library

Labor Defender

June 1932.

Letters between a Scottsboro parent and Tom Mooney's mother.

From A Scottsboro Boy's Mother to Mother Mooney

Atlanta, Ga.

My Dear Friend:

Mrs. Mooney I am riten you a few line to let you hear from me and my little girl Mary Alice. This leves us both well hope you are the same. I mento have rote you before now but just ben pretty bizy. I am making some pillow so if I have to go back north I can take them with me and give them to the comrades to raffil off to help make money for the prisoners. They are mity pretty I think. I do hope I will get to come out there where you are. I sure do think of you often. Not meny days pass I don't think of you.

I sure did hate to read that your son was turn down in getting his pardon. I just get so mad I get sick to think how mean some people are. I am gonter ask the comrades send me out there some time this summer. I sure wood like to be with you one more time in life and if you feel like it you and I can make a few more trips together. I beleive I and you could do good work this summer. See I will leave my little girl here so you think that over. I don't see nothing else for you and I to do but continue to fight until your son Tom and the Scottsboro boys are free.

So I will come to a close, hopen to here from you-all soon, give my love to your sun Tom all so Mrs. Anna hope to here from you soon, from a true friend.

A Scottsboro Mother

(signed) Mrs. Viola Montgomery

70 1/2 McDounagh Blvd.
So. Atlanta, Ga

Reply from Mother Mooney

134 Clipper Street
San Francisco, Calif.

Mrs. Viola Montgomery
70 1/2 McDounagh Blvd.
So. Atlanta, Ga

Dear Mother Montgomery:

I was sure glad to hear from you and your little girl, Mary Alice.

Sure, I was just speaking of you the night before I received your letter and was going to write to get your address. I hope we can both do something for our boys and to work together again to help them.

Last Sunday was May Day and we had a fine parade here. Faith, and I led the parade, wearing the banner, "MY SON IS INNOCENT." They had trucks in the parade, showing an electric chair, the kind they want to use on the Scottsboro boys, and a cell, showing the govenor keeping my boy in jail. Thousands of workers were there cheering for Tom and the Scottboro boys.

Keep cheerful, Mother Montgomery, and keep up the fight as I have for the last sixteen years. I am starting out pretty soon on a new trip with the International Labor Defense. We mothers can do a lot to help our sons. With millions of workers behind us, black and white and all other kinds, ready to fight for your boy and my boy and all other victims of the bosses, we will win this fight yet.

I remain your friend,

MARY MOONEY.

Records of the International Labor Defense, Schomburg Center for Research in Black Culture, New York Public Library

"I Go to Jail for the Scottsboro Boys"

Labor Defender

October 1932.

Ada Wright

I am willing every possible sacrifice to save my two boys, Roy and Andy, from death in the electric chair.

I am not strong. My health has been undermined by life-long and difficult toil. I have brought seven children into the world and did my best for them. I am now more than 46 years old.

It is, therefore, not possible for me to do as much as I would like to save the lives of my two children and the other Scottsboro boys.

I never dreamed that I had the strength to make a seven months tour of the United States and then to cross the Atlantic and for more than four months now to "carry on" in the European Scottsboro campaign.

There have been many difficulties. But my love for my two sons, the overwhelming desire and hope to see them free again, and very soon, with all the Scottsboro boys, with the growing desire, that I did not understand 17 months ago, to achieve something for my people and my class, have kept me strong. I grew to understand the polite attacks upon our meetings. I could even understand my being expelled twice from Belgium, a country which tyrannizes over some many millions of my people in the Congo, in Africa.

But I didn't think that they would ever send me to jail and to prison—just for trying to save the lives of my two sons.

Yet I have been in police stations, jails, and prisons for three long days and endless nights that seemed to me like ages of horrible torture. I have never been in prison for life. I never expected to be. I admit I have a fearful horror of police stations and jails.

Yes, I have been to prison in our struggle to save the Scottsboro boys. And, I will say now that I am willing to go again, and for a longer time if it will help the cause in which so many workers are struggling.

They arrested me at Klodno, in the coal fields near Prague, in Czecho-Slovakia. I had never heard of Czecho-Slovakia, or of Prague, or Klonda, before they were included in our European Scottsboro tour. But the workers here were just like the workers that I saw in the twelve other countries I had visited. One woman comrade who greeted me at Klondo had been a delegate to the Amsterdam Anti-War Congress.

They told me that Klondo was the birthplace of Anthony J. Cermak, the Democratic mayor of Chicago. He had been to Klondo only a few weeks previously. He had been acclaimed by the government and feasted by its officials. I remember Mayor Cemark's police in Chicago murdered two of my people, shooting them down in the street, during the unemployed demonstration against the eviction from their homes of some jobless Negro workers. I have heard much more about the police terror in Chicago.

That makes it easier for me to understand why I should be arrested by the friends of the Chicago's mayor in Klondo, over here in Czecho-Slovakia in Europe.

I was arrested before I ever spoke at or even reached the Klondo meeting. They dragged me off to the police station and tried to terrorize me into admitting that I was trying to carry on Communist propaganda. They tried to get me to say that I intended talking "politics," and that I was trying to interfere with the local conditions in Klondo. I told them I didn't know anything about conditions in Klondo, that I didn't know enough yet to talk about politics, and that I felt I didn't know enough yet about Communism to be a good Communist.

At first they said they would release me after the meeting, which went on without me, was over. But they lied. They announced instead they would lock me up for the night. I demanded the right to go to a hotel and said I would pay for it with my own money.

This they refused me. It was one o'clock in the morning when they put me into a cell and locked me up.

Some of the comrades had remained close to me all this time. But they were forced at last to say, "Good Night!"

At that moment I never felt so much alone in all my life. I admit that I really broke down and cried. But in that very same moment I resolved not to shed a tear in any boss class jail or prison. And I didn't although the two nights following were even worse than the first.

Sunday night I spent in Prague police station fighting off the bugs and vermin. I shall never forget. And the next day, Labor Day in the United States, September 5, I was taken to the Fispann Prison where deportees are interned before being sent out of the country. Instead of releasing me, the interior minister, through his own paper called me a "Bolshevik Negro Woman," in big headline, and "A Black Communist."

But the women in the prison just loved me. I divided with them all the things the comrades brought me. The comrades gave me money to buy things to eat, whatever I needed. But the prison officials got their hands on the money and kept it.

So on the fourth day they sent me out of the country with Comrade Engdahl, declaring we were "undesirable foreigners."

Going to prison for the first time has started me thinking about many things. The police accompanied us on the train as far as Austrian border to see that we were safely out of the country.

The Austrian comrades greeted us at Vienna and began arranging meetings to take place of those denied us in Czecho-Slovakia.

And I see that the newspaper everywhere is discussing the action of the Czechoslovakian government and the Scottsboro campaign. Perhaps I did not go to prison in vain.

Records of the International Labor Defense, Schomburg Center for Research in Black Culture, New York Public Library

"Whose Supreme Court?"

Labor Defender

November 1932.

Cyril Briggs

Nine old men, sitting in the highest court of American capitalism, faced on October 10 the necessity of deciding whether it would be safe to uphold the hideous Scottsboro legal lynch verdicts in the face of the angry thunder of protest from workers and intellectuals throughout the world, and the rising resistance of the Negro (some word I cannot read) to the capitalist lynch terror. The court has, not yet announced its decision.

The historic class forces which have clashed in countless battles around the Scottsboro Case during the past 18 months were well represented at the October 10 hearing before the United States Supreme Court. These forces filed into the court in two opposing streams. From their conspiratorial chambers came the nine old men of the Supreme Court, togged out in sartorial devices aimed at enhancing their dignity. From entrances set aside for the privileged representatives of the capitalist class, including a large delegation of Alabama Congressmen and other members of the minority of white landlords and landowners exercising a bloody rule over the "Black Belt." Congress was not in session, and most of its members were touring their districts peddling their pre-election lies and sham promises, but the Alabama contingent in congress was on hand to demonstrate its solidarity with the Alabama lynch courts which had rushed nine innocent Negro children through a farcical trial to death sentences for eight and—for effect—a mistrial for the ninth.*

These representatives of the Alabama ruling class seated themselves around Thomas E. Knight, Jr., Alabama Attorney General who was present to oppose the appeal argued by the International Labor Defense attorneys and to defend the lynch verdicts. Knight's father, a member of the Alabama Supreme

---

*The International Labor Defense attorneys, supported by the world-wide mass protest, had later forced the Alabama Supreme Court to admit the existence of irregularities in the trial of Eugene Williams, one of the eight originally convicted to death, and had ordered a new trial for this boy. The majority opinion upheld the lynch verdicts for the other seven.. In a dissenting opinion, the Chief Justice of the Alabama Supreme Court was forced to admit that none of the boys had received a fair trial.

Court, had previously concurred in the majority opinion of that court upholding the lynching verdicts. Seated with the Alabama group was also former United States Senator Thomas J. Heflin, notorious Negro-baiter.

Opposing these forces of capitalist reaction were hundreds of Washington Negro and white workers who had got into the court room past the hostile challenges of a heavy police guard specially called out for the occasion. The newspapers reported that the entire Washington police force had been mobilized in fear of hostile demonstrations by workers against lynch verdicts and the United States Supreme Court. These workers were there to show their solidarity with the Scottsboro victims of capitalist justice, their resentment against the murderous frame-up of those working class children, and finally their support of the arguments of the battery of famous attorneys engaged by the International Labor Defense for the oral argument before the court.

This solidarity of the white workers of the whole world with the persecuted Negro masses was dramatically demonstrated in the court room itself, with the entrance of Mother Mooney, mother of Tom Mooney, victim of another notorious frame-up by the American ruling-class. A flunky of capitalism in the person of the U.S. Marshall attempted to bar Mrs. Mooney from the hearing on the grounds that she could have no interest in Scottsboro Case and the fate of the nine Negro lads. Mother Mooney who, in the company of Richard B. Moore, Negro proletarian orator, had traveled thousands of miles throughout the United States, in defiance of the orders of her physician, for the Scottsboro-Mooney defense campaign, brushed aside the arguments of the U.S. Marshall. She was permitted to remain.

The high court of capitalism was definitely on the defensive. It had felt the impact of the thunderous mass protests welling up from all corners of the world. It sensed the breaking down of the capitalist-erected barriers between the white and Negro masses. The cry of millions of workers against the lynch-justice was ringing in its ears. It realized that Scottsboro had become the symbol of working class unity against the bloody rule of the dying capitalist system, against the savage persecution of the Negro nation in the "Black Belt."

In the three cases preceding the Scottsboro argument, the justices took an active part in questioning the attorneys on both sides. In the Scottsboro Case they maintained a studied silence. This silence was in sharp contrast to their animated interest in two liquor cases, in which they were greatly concerned on questions such as for what number of days a search warrant in a liquor case was good, and whether it was necessary to have an affidavit in order to renew it. Quite clearly, the justices were afraid to ask questions in the Scottsboro Case, both for fear of dramatizing the fundamental issues of Negro rights involved, and for fear of revealing their hatred and hostility toward the Negro masses and the entire working-class. Their antagonism toward the Negro masses was clearly exposed, however, in one of the liquor cases in which one of the attorneys was a Negro. Both Justices McReynolds and Sutherland openly showed their resentment at the appearance of a Negro lawyer before court, bullying and baiting him throughout the hearing. In the Scottsboro hearing, however, all the enthusiasm of the justices for the liquor cases had vanished.

Walter Pollak, who argued the case for the I.L.D., forcefully exposed the facts of the frame-up of the nine boys, masterfully presenting the evidence proving that the boys were not granted a trial, "were denied due process of law," were given no time to prepare their defense, were not permitted to communicate with their parents, although all of the boys were minors; that the very defense lawyers foisted by the Scottsboro court on the boys had failed to call a single defense witness, had never opened or closed to the juries, had not consulted with the parents of the boys and made no proper preliminary motions, that the boys were tried, convicted and sentenced to death in less than two weeks.

He declared that the boys would have had proper attorneys had they been granted time to prepare their defense, and in proof, he pointed to the fact that they were later ably represented by General George W. Chamlee (a Southern attorney engaged by the International Labor Defense, who laid the basis for the appeal to the Supreme Court).

Justice McReynolds, who had listened with an air of boredom to the argument of the I.L.D. attorney, immediately pricked up his ears and leaned forward when the Alabama Attorney General Knight opened his defense of the lynch sentences. So did Heflin and the delegation of Alabama congressmen presented. Knight argued that the Alabama Supreme Court had reviewed the sentences and had declared them to be just and made the significant statement that the Alabama justices know their local problems. He had no apology for the severity of the sentences, he declared, with an approving nod from Supreme Justice McReynolds. Launching into a demagogic defense of Alabama lynch justice, he declared that Alabama regards with great jealousy the rights of a defendant, adding "regardless of race or color." He denied that the trials were conducted in an atmosphere of lynch terror, passing over the demonstrations of the mob hailing the first lynch verdicts of the jury which reached a disagreement in the case of the ninth boy, Roy Wright.

No illusions! The Supreme Court belongs to the ruling class as completely as the courts in Alabama. Only class justice can be expected from this sancta sanctorum of Wall Street government! Only mass pressure—mass protests on a swiftly increasing scale—will free the Scottsboro boys—will save them from the electric chair! The Scottsboro boys must not burn! We demand their unconditional freedom!

Records of the International Labor Defense, Schomburg Center for Research in Black Culture, New York Public Library

"Manifesto to the Negro People"

Labor Defender

November 1932.

William L. Patterson
  Negro Workers, Farmers and Intellectuals:
  The attacks upon the Negro people are growing.

Mob violence, lynch terror and jim-crowism are everywhere on the increase. These are the special forms of persecution for us who are Negroes. We who occupy the lowest level of the social ladder.

This terrorization, together with the increasing burdens of mass unemployment, the cutting of our wages to the bone, the totally inadequate relief, or in most cases none at all, tremendous prices for food as a result of all these—mass starvation make our situation an unbearable nightmare of misery and degradation.

During the past three years of the crisis, the terror against us has risen to higher levels and taken on more varied forms. The changed economic and political conditions of this period of hard times, presents to those in power a more difficult task in hiding their leading role in our persecution.

Before, it was more easy for them to place the blame of outrages against us at the door of the white workers. Today, the unity between Negro workers growing out of our common misery and oppression, is developing as never before and forces the ruling class in their determination to "divide and rule" to intensify their efforts to pit one section of the working class against another.

Before, violence against us took the form of illegal lynching of individual Negroes by lynch mobs slyly provoked into murderous action by the ruling class and of individual, though numerous cases of jim-crowism. Now to this form of murderous attack and jim-crowism, they have added attempted legal lynchings on such a scale as Scottsboro and Logan Circle, Washington, the burning of whole Negro sections of a town as in Oklahoma, the massacre of enslaved share-croppers as in Camp Hill, Alabama, the most brutal and vicious murder of whole negro families as the family Judge Crawford in Sanatopia, Miss.

Now the press of the ruling class openly provokes and incites rioting against us as in the Euel Lee case in Baltimore, Scottsboro and Camp Hill. The crisis of capitalism has brought the ruling class of America in protection of its profits into the open against us. Brazenly it declares "Open Season," no license required for hunting and murdering Negroes.

Why are we so viciously attacked now?

In order that the profit system which has held us in slavery for more then three hundreds of years shall continue. Capitalism grown fat at our expense would save itself at our expense.

The burdens of the crisis are being crowded down on the back of the working class, but they rest most heavily upon us who are on the bottom.

Prostitution, disease and suicides increase among us. The government gives relief only to the great banks, railroads, and other big industries, unemployment and social insurance are denied to us.

Evictions for non-payment of rent, the shutting off of gas, water and electricity are daily occurrences where poverty-stricken Negroes are concerned. Those thrown in the streets must go homeless and hungry that capitalism may live.

The masses of our people on the land are dehumanized, their positions often worse then that of the animals with which they work.

These are for us questions of life and death. We must defend ourselves. There is no alternative. We can no longer be guided by those who demand our reliance upon courts, the jim-crow character of whose decisions are known before hand.

But we need not seek to defend ourselves alone! Against our strength, the forces of reaction would be tremendous. We must seek to ally ourselves with those in American life whose conditions approach our own.

Fifteen millions of American working class are today unemployed. The overwhelming majority of these are white workers. Tens of thousands of them are starving.

Already in the struggle for food in England, Arkansas, in the coal miners strike against wage-cuts and worsening conditions on the job, in the internationally known Scottsboro case, we have learned that the unity of Negro and white workers offers the only possibility of success against the attempts of the ruling class to crush us all. Tremendous battles have been waged wherever Negroes and white workers have begun a struggle for their lives.

These battles have been fought in the streets and in the courts of the ruling class. The measure of our success has been determined by the extent of our unity.

These struggles must be carried to a higher level, this unity must be made international. There is no other way out.

The terror against us becomes more vicious now in order to smash the developing unity between us and white workers, to crush our ever increasing will to resist and to create among us such a degree of terror as will make the placing of the burdens of the crisis upon our shoulders an easy task.

There is one organization that takes a leading place in these defense struggles, that guides and directs them and that is built up out of our own strength and the strength of those who sympathize with us,—this is the International Labor Defense.

It is building a wall of defense around those leaders of ours whom by imprisonment the ruling class would keep from the ranks of struggle.

The forward march of Negro and white workers into the struggle for the solution of the crisis in the interest of the working class demands a forward march of Negro and white workers in the battalions of defense.

We must organize into a united front of defense of all workers in the factories, in our neighborhoods, our lodges, fraternal organizations and mass demonstrations of protest against police brutality and terror. We must look forward to the launching of an irresistible attack upon the whole system of lynching of jim-crowism and special persecution against us. This is a united front struggle for an attack upon the whole.

This united front must extend to all those who are willing fight against boss terror!

Answer the attacks of ruling class of American with the full strength of the Negro and White workers in defense.

Negro Workers! Farmers! Intellectuals! Organize Now!

Harry Haywood Speaks

*O*n November 7, 1932, the United States Supreme Court, by a vote of 7–2, reversed the convictions of the Scottsboro defendants in Powell vs. Alabama. Grounds for reversal were that Alabama failed to provide adequate legal counsel as required by the due process clause of the Fourteenth Amendment. At the same time, demonstrations took place before the Supreme Court in Washington, D.C., in Birmingham, Alabama, and throughout the world.

In response to the positive Supreme Court decision, black Communist Harry Haywood, the Party's foremost theorist on the black self-determination thesis, articulated the Party's response.

Fond 515, Files of the Communist Party of the United States in the Comintern Archives

"The Scottsboro Decision: Victory of Revolutionary Struggle Over Reformist Betrayal"

The Communist

December 1932.

Harry Haywood
The recent action of the United States Supreme Court in reversing the decision of the Scottsboro Circuit Court and the

Alabama Supreme Court in the Scottsboro case, is a victory of far-reaching significance in the struggles of the Negro masses for liberation and the revolutionary labor movement in general. The powerful mass protest, the Communist Party and the International Labor Defense, has again stayed the hands of the Alabama lynchers in carrying through their sinister designs to murder the innocent Negro boys. The decision of the Supreme Court is further proof and vindication of the correctness of the revolutionary policy of the Communist Party.

At the same time, the decision of the Supreme Court was calculated to revive the confidence of the masses in the bourgeois-democratic institutions. The democratic illusions of the masses, already shaken by the crisis and the boss offensive, have been further undermined by the movement of mass action and political exposure carried through by the Communist Party and International Labor Defense around the case of the Scottsboro boys. The New York *Times*, reactionary organ of finance capital, emphasizes just this fact. The decision, it states, is not—

> due to the outcry in Washington and in other cities, as well as in Moscow and by European Communists, asserting that a spirit of wicked class prejudice pervades the United States, and that here no justice can be had for the poor and ignorant. . . . That great tribunal (the United States Supreme Court) appears once more as mindful of human rights. It is not often that we see the issue of justice to the lowliest and possibly the most unworthy, so clearly appearing in an important judicial decision. It ought to abate the rancor of extreme radicals, while confirming the faith of the American people in the soundness of their institutions and especially in the integrity of their courts.

To "abate" the anger of the masses, to confirm their faith in the "soundness" of bourgeois institutions "especially in the integrity of the courts"—this then was [the] avowed object of the decision. Thus, in the same breath while denying the role of the mass movement and attacking the communist Party, the capitalists are nevertheless forced to admit that in making their decision the motive of the honorable gentlemen of the supreme court was to allay the mass movement. Thus the strategy of the imperialists is clear, heralding the decision as a vindication of "justice" to confuse and disarm the vigilance of the masses, and in this manner to lay the ground for a new attack.

Only in the light of the mass movement can the decision of the United States Supreme Court be understood.

Let us look at the decision. Even a cursory examination of this lengthy document despite the befogging terminology in which it is couched, shows that in it the fundamental political questions involved in the case are contemptuously brushed aside and that the decision is based entirely upon legal technicalities.

> The only one of the assignments which we shall consider is the second, in respect of the denial of counsel: *and it becomes unnecessary to discuss the facts of the case or the circumstances surrounding the prosecution* except insofar as they reflect light upon that question.

Thus the frame-up character of the case, the savage lynch atmosphere surrounding and dominating the trial, the barring of Negroes from the jury—all of these fundamental questions raised by the defense, which bespeak the barbarous national oppression of the negro people, the flagrant denial of even the most elementary rights, were brazenly ignored in the Supreme Court decision.

Under cover upholding "democracy," "constitutional rights," the Supreme Court endorses the violation of democratic rights for the Negro masses as reflected in Scottsboro.

But this is not all. The Supreme Court gives the cue to the Alabama lynchers on how such matters should be handled in this period of the political awakening of the toilers. It tells the Alabama lynchers that it has no objection to the legal murder of these innocent boys, provided it is carried through with the due observance of bourgeois legal forms. Felix Frankfurter, the "great liberal," in the New York *Times* of November 13, frankly admits that—

> It (Supreme Court decision) leaves that fate (the murder of the boys) ultimately untouched. Upon the question of guilt or innocence it bears not even remotely. That question remains to be determined in normal course by the constituted tribunals of Alabama. *The Supreme Court has declared only that the determination must be made with due observance of the decencies of civilized procedures.*

That Alabama slave-drivers lose no time in picking up the cue. Through their mouthpiece, the *Birmingham Post*, they hasten to give assurance that—

> Every precaution should be taken so that no room is left for criticism and twisting of fact when the second trials have been completed and the verdict is pronounced.

The decision of the Supreme Court reflects once again the solid united front of Wall Street finance capital with the Southern slave-drivers to maintain national opposition of the Negro people.

Political Background of the Scottsboro Case

Scottsboro is but a single expression of the whole system of national oppression of the Negro people—a system which in this country of "enlightened" capitalist democracy holds in shameless suppression a nation of 14,000,000 human beings, subjects them to super-exploitation on the plantation and in the factories, through a system of segregation and Jim-Crowism, denies them even the most elementary political rights and relegates them to a position of social pariahs.

The Scottsboro frame-up, taking place in the midst of the crisis and deepening revolutionary ferment of the masses, dramatizes in all its harshness the brutal character of the imperialist offensive as directed particularly against the Negro masses. Scottsboro raised in the most acute manner fundamental questions affecting the lives of the Negro masses: lynching, peonage, Jim-Crowism, denial of human rights—the whole system of national oppression, which, as a result of the crisis, has undergone an all-round worsening.

Scottsboro also revealed the growing movement among the Negro toilers in the factories and on the plantations, the forerunners of the gathering struggles for Negro liberation, for land and freedom. Scottsboro revealed how the ruling class hopes to maintain this system under conditions of deepening crisis, growing struggle and unity of Negro and white toilers. This policy of the white ruling class received its most open and brutal expression in the statement of Governor Ross Sterling of Texas. In refusing the stay of execution in the case of a framed-up young Negro, this arrogant spokesman of the slave-drivers stated, *"It may be that this boy is innocent. But it is sometimes necessary to burn a house in order to save a village."*

Obviously, the "village" which Governor Sterling and those whom he represents seek to save, is the system of national oppression of the Negro people threatened by the rising revolt of the Negro toilers against landlord-capitalist slavery, which was so clearly symbolized in the case of the young Negro farmhand. This shows that mob violence and legal lynchings are all part of the capitalist methods of suppression in the attempt to intimidate and terrorize the Negro masses and to split the growing unity of the Negro and white toilers.

The Communist Party proceeded from the basic understanding of the Scottsboro case as a part of the national oppression of the Negro masses—not merely a case of nine boys but a case of nine *Negro* boys, persecuted as members of an oppressed people. Hence, the struggle for the complete freedom of the Scottsboro boys could be effective only if linked up with the struggle against the whole system which breeds similar Scottsboros, and by involving in this struggle the broadest masses of Negro and white toilers. To make Scottsboro a decisive battle on the whole front of Negro liberation—such was the aim of the party.

The tactics of the Communist Party were: no reliance on the capitalist courts, the instruments of national and class oppression; on the contrary it carried on the sharpest fight against all democratic and legalistic illusions among the masses. While utilizing all legal and parliamentary possibilities, adequate legal aid to the victims, petitions, etc., it subordinated these to the organization and development of revolutionary mass action outside of courts and bourgeois legislative bodies.

Only on the basis of such revolutionary tactics could the Communist Party develop a mass movement around Scottsboro, drawing into support of this movement all of the oppressed classes. Only through such methods, did we succeed in staying the murder of the innocent victims.

Revolutionary Tactics Versus Reformist Betrayals

In the course of the development of the struggle for the Scottsboro boys, and as the movement gained momentum, there took place a crystallization of class forces. The revolutionary tactics of the Communist Party forced out in the open all enemies of the working class and the Negro people. A constellation of all the reactionary forces, extending from the white imperialists, the Ku Klux Klan to the Socialists and Negro reformist lackeys, rapidly began to take form against the movement of the masses, and its leader the Communist Party.

In this reactionary front the division of tasks is and was as follows. The imperialist bourgeoisie through its Southern section was determined to murder the boys as a bloody warning to the Negro masses. Preparing the ground for this, it attempted to incite the wildest chauvinist passions among the masses of white people. This aim was supplemented by the Socialist and Negro bourgeois reformist agents, whose task was to confuse and disorganize the revolutionary defense movement within, by fostering illusions as to the "fairness and impartiality" of bourgeois courts and institutions and attacking the Communist Party.

In this a most important role was assigned to the Negro reformists grouped around the National Association for the Advancement of Colored People. At first the N.A.A.C.P. completely ignored the case. Forced finally by the mass protest to take a stand on the case, it issued its first press release. The *Crisis*, organ of the N.A.A.C.P. in an attempt to explain away this treachery writes:

> "When we hear that eight colored men have raped two white girls in Alabama we are not the first in the field to defend them. *If they were guilty and had a fair trail* the case is none of our business. We did not know whether they were guilty or not. We feared an unjust trail even if they were guilty. But first we sought the facts, we must have the truth. Once we were convinced that the eight ignorant, poverty stricken boys had been framed by a mob on the forced testimony of two prostitutes, then and not until then did we throw every ounce of energy into the Scottsboro case."

The statement that the boys were framed up by a mob is a deliberate lie. The obvious purpose of this mis-statement is to shift the responsibility for the lynch verdicts from the courts and the white ruling class, onto the masses, thereby helping the Alabama slave-drivers to conceal the lynch character of their institutions. This, of course, is in keeping with the main task of these Negro misleaders, to bolster up the illusions of the masses in the institutions of the ruling class lynchers. This is also witnessed in the statement "we feared an unjust trial" which infers that it is possible for the boys to receive "impartial justice" at the hands of the lynchers themselves.

After this it is clear that the only factor that really "convinced" the N.A.A.C.P. was the rising movement of the Negro and white toilers against the vicious frame-up which seriously threatened its leadership over the Negro masses. It was precisely this movement that "convinced" the N.A.A.C.P. "to throw every ounce of energy into the Scottsboro case," however, not against the lynchers of the Negro people, but against those forces organizing and leading the mass movement for the defense of the boys—the Communist Party and the International Labor Defense.

Thus on May 8, claiming that there "were strong grounds for believing the boys innocent," the N.A.A.C.P. is alarmed by the fact "that the Communist sympathizers actually sent telegrams to the Sheriff and Governor demanding the immediate unconditional release of the boys, a thing which neither was empowered to do." Again, on May 11, the N.A.A.C.P. characterized the demand for the immediate unconditional release of the boys as a "manifestly absurd and impossible demand," adding that "The Communists, however, seem far more interested in making Communist propaganda out of this case than they are in genuinely trying to save the boys from the electric chair."

Continuing this line on May 16, the Pittsburgh *Courier*, mouthpiece of the N.A.A.C.P. which in the first days of the case called the boys "rapists," openly attacking the Communist Party, stated:

> "It is more likely, however, that if mobs break out in Alabama and these eight boys are taken from the chair and lynched, it would probably be due to the nonsensical activities of the Communists, who by their misguided energies are finally driving the citizens of Alabama to the point of desperation."

Thus the lynchers are not only completely absolved from any responsibility for the fate of the boys, but are actually justified in their lynch terror against the Negro people. It follows, according to this, that in order to save the nine boys, the main fire must be directed against the Communists and the mass protest movement under their leadership.

The Alabama Ku Klux Klan, recognized the valuable support to its lynch policy, correctly stated through its organ, the

Jackson County *Sentinel,* that there was no principle difference between the N.A.A.C.P. and the Southern ruling class.

Logically developing this line, the N.A.A.C.P. misleaders joined with the lynchers in open provocation against the mass protest movement and its leader, the Communist Party. In a speech in Chattanooga, William Pickens, Field Organizer of the N.A.A.C.P. warned the southern capitalists.

> Let the white people of Alabama sit up and take notice: this Communist sapping through the densely ignorant portion of the colored population, while not immediately menacing to government itself, is certainly menacing to good race relations.

It is significant to note that this speech of Pickens openly inciting the lynchers to violence against the masses, was made on the eve of the battle at Camp Hill when the Alabama bourgeoisie attempted to crush the first organized expression of the developing struggle of the sharecroppers and the inauguration of a campaign of terror in the lower South which according even to the imperialist agent, Howard Kester of the Fellowship of Reconciliation, resulted in the murder of seventy-five Negroes. Undoubtedly, this speech placed an additional weapon in the hands of the white ruling class against the Negro people.

It was by these methods that the N.A.A.C.P. leaders attempted to disorganize the revolutionary mass movement, isolate the Communist Party and the revolutionary organizations and furnish a cloak behind which the Alabama lynchers could carry through their bloody work. In brief, their attacks were directed not against the violence and lynch terror of the capitalists, but against the resistance of the masses. Truly, in Scottsboro the N.A.A.C.P. played the role of assistant hangman of Negro masses.

The despicable treachery of the Negro bourgeois reformists, their cringing servility to the white ruling class as exemplified in the Scottsboro case, is not accidental, but represents the basic tendency of Negro reformism as based upon the peculiar position of the Negro bourgeoisie, and the inevitable development of this tendency under conditions of sharpening crisis and rise of Negro liberation and working class struggles.

"Holy Alliance" of the Socialist Party and Negro Reformists

The Socialist Party fully supported and complemented the activities of the Negro reformists. Thus, Thomas, the chief exponent of American "Socialism," wrote in the *New Leader* of April 2, 1932:

> "The Communist tactics of exploiting labor struggles and examples of racial injustice for Party purposes probably helps to explain the action of the Alabama Supreme Court in confirming the conviction of the Scottsboro boys."

Mr. Thomas gloatingly hails the decision of the Alabama Supreme Court, upholding the lynch verdict of the lower courts as a vindication of reformist tactics of reliance on the institutions of the ruling class oppressors as against the mass struggles. In this he would have the workers believe that the poor Alabama lynchers were deterred from their "noble" and "humane" efforts to give the boys a "fair" and "impartial" trial by the tactics of the Communist Party. Of course, even this act of the lynchers (so Mr. Thomas pretends) is merely an isolated case of "miscarriage of justice" and not a part of the whole system of oppression, terror and lynching of the Negro people.

Undoubtedly, Mr. Thomas is opposed to the Communist tactics of mass revolutionary struggles for the freedom of the boys on the same ground that he is opposed to the entire struggle for Negro national liberation as expressed in the slogan he says "at best it *suggests segregation* for the Negro tenth of our population, at worst it invites *race war.*" Why does Mr. Thomas seek to identify the slogans of right of self-determination with the imperialist policy of segregation, a policy directed to enforcing the isolation of the Negro people as a condition for preserving their economic, social and political inequality? It is clear that in the Black Belt the struggle against segregation is bound up with and is a part of the struggle for the revolutionary overthrow of the capitalist land-owners' dictatorship in this territory, the establishment of the right of the Negro majority to determine their own fate without force-ful interference from without, to set up their own state institutions (administrative, legislative, etc.) corresponding to the need of the majority of the population. This means the confiscation of the land of the big white landlords and capitalists (the material basis of their power over the Negro masses) in favor of the toilers, the establishment of the state unity of the Black Belt under the rule and in keeping with the interests of the Negro people, and with-drawal of the armed forces of the white imperialist ruling class from this Negro territory. This is the real meaning of the right of self-determination. Only through the struggle for the realization of this demand can an end be put to the imperialist policy of segre-gation. It is clear, therefore, that the purpose of Mr. Thomas in identifying the slogan of the right of self-determination with the imperialist policy of segregation is to sow confusion in the ranks of the Negro and white toilers and in this manner hinder the real struggle against segregation.

This same purpose is carried a step further by Mr. Thomas in his contention that "this slogan invites race war." There can be no doubt that what Mr. Thomas is pleased to call "race war" is in actuality the national liberation war of the Negro people against segregation and all forms of national oppression, i.e., the struggle for equal rights and the right of self-determination in the Black Belt. Therefore by the use of the bourgeois term "race war" he attempts to interpret the national rebellion of the Negro peoples for land and freedom, not as a struggle of the Negro masses supported by the revolutionary white working class, but as a struggle between the Negro people on one side and the whole white people on the other side. In this Mr. Thomas accepts completely the bourgeois race theory of immutable antagonisms between Negroes and whites, including the workers of both races. It follows that in order to avert "race wars" the Negro people must accept lynching, jim-crowism, etc., and on the other hand, the white workers must not support the struggles of the Negro masses. Thus by obscuring the real class essence of the Negro national liberation movement, Mr. Thomas seeks to confuse the workers, perpetuate the division between Negro and white toilers, and strengthen white chauvinism. In this demagogic formula, there is again revealed the Socialist program on the Negro question, which rejects the struggle for Negro rights on the ground that this struggle is inimical to the interests of the working class. Under the hypocritical cloak of pretending to be opposed to segregation, Mr. Thomas and the Socialist Party endorse the white slave-drivers' status quo of lynching and oppression of the Negro people. Inasmuch as the mass movement organized and led by the Communist Party constitutes a serious threat to this outrageous system, it is quite natural that Mr. Thomas should be found on the side of the lynchers and against the masses.

Against this reactionary united front of imperialist slave drivers and their Negro and white reformist lackeys the Communist Party alone stands out as the only force championing, organizing and leading the struggles of the Negro people and white toilers against national oppression and for the overthrow of the system which breeds lynchings and Scottsboros.

The struggle for the lives of the Scottsboro boys shows clearly who are the friends and who are the enemies of the Negro people. Scottsboro strengthened the differentiation among the Negro reformists, thus tremendously increasing the revolutionary experience of the Negro masses. Scottsboro marks a further step in the achievement of the revolutionary hegemony of the proletariat and the leadership of the Communist Party, in the Negro liberation movement. Scottsboro, by drawing millions of toilers, Negroes and whites, into a struggle for Negro rights, is a great step forward in the education of the workers in a spirit of working class internationalism. Thus, Scottsboro stands out as an historic landmark in the liberation movement of the Negro people and in the revolutionary labor movement in general.

Next Steps in Scottsboro

The series of partial victories in the battle for the unconditional release of the Scottsboro boys, and particularly the latest victory, is complete vindication of the effectiveness of revolutionary mass struggle to defeat the attempts of the bourgeoisie to carry through its drive of terror and suppression. But this must not be constructed to mean that the struggle is already over. Now more than ever before it is necessary to strengthen and broaden the ranks of solidarity of the Negro and white toilers. Now more than ever before, it is necessary to enlist new fighters, new blood, new masses, to compel the instruments of reaction to hand over the Scottsboro boys unharmed and untouched. It is essential, both politically and organizationally, to strengthen a hundred fold the united front of the masses as the only guarantee for the complete freedom of the Negro boys.

In this, we must sharpen the character of fight against an exposure of the Socialist leaders and Negro reformists, as the main social supports of imperialist Jim-Crow reaction in the ranks of the Negro and white toilers. In regard to the Negro reformists, we must guard against two mistakes which have been manifested in the Scottsboro campaign and in the struggle against lynching. The first is the underestimation of the class role of Negro reformism. This arises from failure to distinguish clearly between the national reformist tendency as based upon the Negro bourgeoisie and its alliance with the imperialist ruling classes, on the one hand, and, on the other hand, the national revolutionary tendency of the Negro masses against the oppression of white ruling classes. It was this mistake which, especially in the fist stages of the Scottsboro struggle, led to a tendency to lag at the tail of the Negro bourgeois reformists, as witnessed particularly in the failure to expose their "left" agents among masses, such as Pickens, to anticipate the inevitable betrayal of these fakers and to prepare the masses for this betrayal. This mistake led to a whole series of errors in our strategy and tactics in the Scottsboro campaign, which, in the main, were as follows: tendency to resist the political broadening out and deepening of the campaign by systematically linking it up with the general and specific economic and political demands of the Negro people and the working class; a hesitancy in bringing forth and popularizing our full Negro program (self-determination, equal rights, confiscation of land), in the course of the Scottsboro campaign. This underestimation of Negro reformism was glaringly manifested in the "united front from the top" maneuvers with petty-bourgeois leaders of Negro mass organizations, "friendly" ministers, and so forth, leading to a situation in many places where the mass movement, to a certain extent, was left to the mercies of these agents of the bourgeoisie.

The second mistake consists in the mechanical identification of the Negro reformists with the ruling imperialist bourgeoisie. This is revealed in the tendency to replace real political exposure of the Negro reformists by vulgar name-calling and noisy phrases.

On the basis of relentless struggle against both of these deviations, coupled with the correct political exposure of the Negro reformists, it is necessary to at once establish the broadest united front of all elements among the Negro and white peoples ready to fight for the freedom of the Scottsboro boys. We must carry the struggle for the Scottsboro boys outside the narrow periphery of the I.L.D. and our mass revolutionary organizations, greatly widening its organizational base to include even the most backward masses of toilers. Scottsboro committees must be set up in the neighborhoods, with particular emphasis on the Negro neighborhoods, in factories, particularly where large numbers of Negroes are employed, in Jim-Crow schools, etc.

These elementary united front organizational forms have been historically proven to be the most effective in rallying the widest masses in the struggles around burning issues, for the development of the initiative and self-activity of the masses. Organized on the basis of struggle for the Scottsboro boys these committees in the course of broadening out the movement through the systematic introduction of other immediate issues confronting the Negro masses, can become the basis for more permanent organizations— unemployed block committees, factory and shop organizations.

This line of development was shown clearly in the initial stages of the Scottsboro campaign where the Scottsboro defense committees, organized on the basis of neighborhoods, actually became the basis in many places for building up of the unemployed movement among the Negroes.

At the same time, the revolutionary mass organizations under the leadership of the Party and the I.L.D. must become the main driving force in this united front and must be drawn into more active participation by setting up Scottsboro committees in their own organizations to initiate and broaden the work among the masses of workers under their leadership linked up with the issues confronting these workers.

The further development of the struggle for the release of the Scottsboro boys must be linked up more effectively with the struggle against Negro persecution in all localities as well as with the struggle against the general capitalist offensive. Scottsboro must be brought into every action of the working class against the offensive—strikes, unemployed demonstrations, farmers' struggles, etc.

With the shifting back of the fate of the boys to the Alabama courts, the struggle for their release must have as its major point of concentration—the South. The unemployed movement in Birmingham, the development of the cropper's movement in the lower South, the struggles against the terror, offer us the base for a real mass fight right in the very area of the lynch courts.

The Scottsboro defense must be raised to a higher level of activity and organization and must be used as a rallying point for the development of a tremendous nation-wide mass movement against lynching as a vital link in the struggle for national liberation of the Negro people, and in the winning of the masses for the revolutionary counter-offensive against the imperialist bourgeoisie.

William Patterson Speaks

Records of the International Labor Defense, Schomburg Center for Research in Black Culture, New York Public Library
The Scottsboro Decision: An Analysis

January 1933.

Wm. L. Patterson, National Secretary I.L.D.

An analysis of the Southern Case is vitally necessary. This, to be complete, must treat of the political significance of Scottsboro, its strength as an organizational vehicle and as an educational platform. It must treat of the possibilities this case contains for destroying the illusions of democracy. It must struggle against the deeply rooted anti-Negro prejudices of the white workers and it must wage a systematic fight against the natural distrust of the Negro masses.

Scottsboro exposes the present and constantly shifting array of class forces in America. The Scottsboro defense blazes a road toward merging the defense struggles of American workers as a whole with the defense of the fighters for Negro liberation. Without this merger no successful defense struggles can be waged. It discloses the correctness of the demands raised by the defense for full economic, political, and social equality for the Negro masses and for the right for self-determination in the Black Belt. The correctness of the defense methods of the International Labor Defense reveals the revolutionary contents of the Scottsboro Case. Scottsboro is a revolutionary arsenal.

Scottsboro marks a historical forward step in revolutionary defense struggles in America. Here we will deal with the one phase of the court decision in the Scottsboro case.

Before the Scottsboro case went to the first trial the Jackson County (ALA) *Sentinel* wrote: "Calm thinking citizens last night revealed that while this was the most atrocious crime charged in our country, that the evidence against the Negroes was so conclusive as to be almost perfect and that the ENDS OF JUSTICE can be best secured by a legal process (*emphasis mine—WLP*)."

This is clearly an instruction that outright lynching is not necessary, and that the court will take care of the affair. The "perfect evidence" was the testimony of two women whom police records showed to be notorious prostitutes. The call for a legal lynching was openly based upon this. Behind this, however, stood the necessity of extending to the white workers the possibility of engaging in terror against the Negro masses in conjunction with the court. This was to smash the growing unity of Negro and white workers in struggle against the increasing burdens of the crisis.

England, Arkansas, testified to the effectiveness of this unity when Negro and white share croppers organized together and took food for their starving families. Its value is shown in the mine struggles in Pennsylvania, West Virginia, and east Ohio, where 40,000 Negro and white miners desperately fought against wage cuts and the worsening of their living conditions. Negroes who were beginning to struggle in demands of full social, political, and economic equality granted by the constitution had to be terrorized. Those who were beginning to understand that full social, political, and economic rights would be granted to the Negro masses only when theirs was the right of self determination—the right to govern themselves—constituted a menace to the continued exploitation of Negro and white workers. Their methods of struggle were destroying the myth of white supremacy and white superiority. In this the crisis helped.

The trial court in Scottsboro proceeded to its task. There were no Negroes on the grand jury which indicted the innocent boys. There were no Negroes on the petit jury which tried them. There were no Negro officials in the court in which they were tried. There were no Negroes in the county acting as officials to secure to prospective jurors. There were no Negro attorneys to take a hand in the trial. Upon the testimony of these two prostitutes, Judge Hawkins based his decision which called for a verdict of guilty.

The jury which tried the first two innocent Negro boys returned its verdict while the jury which was trying another victim of lynch justice was sitting in the jury box, and the prospective jurors who were to try the other six innocent boys sat in the court room. The first verdict was greeted with cheers inside the court room while a mob outside led by a band sang, "There will be a hot time in the old town tonight."

In this atmosphere the trials proceeded. At the same time the National Association for the Advancement of Colored People, which contended that it believed in the innocence of these boys, asked all the workers of America, who demanded for the boys a fair trial, that they placed full reliance on the courts.

It was the attorneys of the International Labor Defense who filed a notice of appeal for these innocent boys who otherwise would have gone to the electric chair on June.10, 1931. The highest court in Alabama faced the same tasks which confronted the trial court; the task of preventing unity of Negro and white workers; the task of maintaining the illusions in the mind of the white workers that they were a part of the so-called white supremacy; the task of defending the myth that the courts were the defenders of white womanhood; the task of aiding the armed forces of the Ku Klux Klan mobs in terrorizing the Negro masses.

Yet in order to prevent Negro masses from clearly seeing that there was no "justice" in these courts for them, the Chief Justice differed in his decision from the legal lynching of these boys. This gesture of the Chief Justice differed in his decision from the controlling opinion which called for the legal lynching of the mass movement which was reaching greater proportions.

Before the case reached the United States Supreme Court, the mass defense had spread to European countries where tens of thousands of workers demanded the immediate, unconditional release of the innocent Scottsboro boys. The European workers saw in the Scottsboro case a force for class solidarity; a force stimulating the revolutionary upsurge of the oppressed and starving masses in the colonial countries. The United States Government sought desperately and unsuccessfully to stop the development of this movement in European countries. It sought to prevent the tour of Mrs. Ada Wright, the unofficial ambassadress of the Negro masses to the European workers and of J. Lewis Engdahl, secretary of the I.L.D.

This movement, the significance of which was recognized by the United States Government, was certainly recognized by its agency, the United States Supreme Court. The pressure of this mass movement forced the decision of the Alabama courts. The United States Supreme court remains "the court of last illusions." None of the issues of the fundamental rights of the Negroes raised by the mass defense and legal defense of the Scottsboro boys were answered by the United States Supreme court. It ignored these in order conform with the lynch courts of the South which of course ignored them. The United States Supreme Court had a difficult and contradictory task to perform, to bolster the waning faith of the Negro and white workers in the illusions of justice in the courts, to get the state courts in the methods of legal lynching, to smash the growing militancy of the Negro masses and to repair their faith in their misleaders who cried put your faith in the courts.

The greatest danger exists that the illusions in the justice of the courts may be deepened by this action of the Supreme Court. The Scottsboro boys will be saved only by the development of even a greater movement than that which now stands behind them. The

International Labor Defense must root itself deep in the ranks of the working class, the workers in the mills, in the shops, in the mines, must be drawn in. They must be called to its ranks to fight against the growing terror. All of the revolutionary content of the Scottsboro case must be exploited to the nth degree.

"The Scottsboro boys shall not die."

"The Scottsboro boys must receive their unconditional freedom and safe conduct to their homes."

Records of the International Labor Defense, Schomburg Center for Research in Black Culture, New York Public Library

"Scottsboro–Our Next Tasks"

Labor Defender

February 1933.

William L. Patterson

The struggle to save the 9 Scottsboro boys has been raised to an extremely high political level. The very government of the United States has become an open participant. It has used its power indiscriminately in an attempt to smash the defense. This is reflected most clearly in its communication with every capitalist European country, where its representatives were instructed: "Stop the mass protest demonstrations for the Scottsboro boys." These demonstrations expose the murderous policy of national oppression which existed in America, exposed the hypocrisy of its lofty declarations of democratic government. The creators of the Scottsboro murder trial have been placed on the defensive and are trying to beat back the outraged protest movement it has aroused.

The European workers further stimulated by the presence of a Scottsboro mother and J. Louis Engdahl, late National Chairman of the International Labor Defense, crowded into the streets in which American consulates and embassies were located, before these to protest the murderous lynch verdict against 9 innocent boys, and the vicious Jim Crow system from which it flowed. Their voices could not be stifled.

In the Soviet Union, where the oppression of innumerable national minorities ended with the October Revolution, the workers and toiling masses, free from police terror, rallied by hundreds of thousands in support of the defense of the Scottsboro boys. It was their experience in fighting against the influence on racial national chauvinism that enabled them to react rapidly and speedily to the defense of the Scottsboro boys.

European workers raised the banner of international working class solidarity high. In the struggle to save the lives of their Negro brothers some of them lost their own, murdered by the police European imperialism sent into the streets in answer to the Wall Street government's damnable directive, but the European workers and sympathizers built stronger their defense organizations in the defense of Scottsboro.

J. Louis Engdahl died a martyr on this front of class struggle. The death of this able leader helped to steel the European workers for greater struggle. But in the United States, where the Scottsboro case was born amid the struggles of the working class and toiling masses against starvation and mass unemployment, we failed to organizationally strengthen the International Labor Defense, our weapon of defense struggles in the heroic struggle.

Why have we failed to fill the ranks of the International Labor Defense when at the same time we have won tremendous influence through Scottsboro? Because we have not penetrated into the masses with Scottsboro. Its flame blinded us to the smaller Scottsboros in every hamlet and every city. It was a magnet which would and did attract tens of thousands, but they saw their own daily defense struggles rather than Scottsboro as an inseparable part of their lives. The hideousness of the crime of Scottsboro detracted our attention from those Scottsboros of lesser magnitude. We did not develop the local defense struggle. These local struggles, these day to day denials of equal rights to the Negro masses, these increasing defense struggles of the whole working class must be linked with Scottsboro. Scottsboro is an inseparable part of them. Merged together greater strength is gained for each.

The struggle to save the innocent Negro boys who for two years have eaten, drunk and slept within sight of the electric chair must be raised to a higher political level. The ruling class sought through the Scottsboro terror to chill the blood of the earth-crushed Negro masses, but their liberation struggles have been raised to a higher level. The toiling Negro masses stand ready to defend their rights, and as in the cases of the Alabama share-croppers, they are defending the rights of the white toiling masses as well. The Scottsboro defense will steel both Negro and white toiling masses as it clears their vision to the forces aligned against them and shows to them their common interests. Scottsboro is pregnant with struggle. Well might the profit-seeking landlords whose dollars drip blood say, "We want no more Scottsboros." Every recent major struggle of the American working class has borne aloft the banner "Save the Scottsboro boys"—and every struggle has thereby gained added strength for itself.

We have got now to find the link that binds our national campaign together. Scottsboro with Mooney, Scottsboro with Tampa—Scottsboro-Mooney-Tampa, the defense of the Alabama share-croppers—these are major defense tasks flowing from the same source of ruling class opposition, but these must be inseparably linked together with local struggles for the tasks of defense can be successfully achieved only if we draw hundreds of thousands of more workers and sympathizers into the struggle as part and parcel of this defense organization.

We must develop a united front of defense around these struggles. Negro reformists, Socialist leaders, renegades—these agents of the ruling class must be isolated from the masses they seek to lead. Freed from this drag upon them the masses must be drawn energetically into the struggle around each case, organized in a defense committee, but it must be a united front committee. It must be formed of all who are willing to fight for that particular issue against which we are struggling. It can well be named for that issue. We must examine each situation, keep our ear to the demands of the masses. There must be no attempt to force upon this committee the entire program of the International Labor

Defense. Gradually, through the correctness of our policy in the united front activities must we prove the correctness of the whole policy of the International Labor Defense.

Our momentary victorious Scottsboro struggle will enable us to go forward to complete victory. The basis has been laid by our activities and the proved correctness of our methods for the development of a mass defense organization. Only our own inner weakness can prevent our realization of this. These weaknesses which are keeping us from the masses must be overcome. We must go to the masses with the story of how our partial victory in the Scottsboro case was won, how our enemies were up to [the] present moment defeated. We must go into the shops, from house to house, among the employed and unemployed workers, the organized and the unorganized, those in reformist and those in revolutionary trade unions, Negro and white, native born and foreign born, young and old.

The Communist members of the International Labor Defense must understand that the International Labor Defense is not a Communist organization, must recognize that he is the best Communist whose activities best enable that organization of which he is a part to function to reach the masses, to clarify the masses as to their interests, to draw them into struggle.

Free all of the class war prisoners!

Build the I.L.D. in struggle!

Records of the International Labor Defense, Schomburg Center for Research in Black Culture, New York Public Library

"We Indict the Alabama Lynchers"

Labor Defender

March 1933.

William L. Patterson

"The ugly demand or threat from outsiders that Alabama reverse its jury decision and the FILTHY INSINUATIONS THAT OUR PEOPLE ARE MURDERERS when they were sincerely being as fair as ever in the history of the country IS RATHER STRAINING ON OUR IDEA OF FAIR PLAY."—(Emphasis, W.L.P.)

Thus wrote the Jackson County *Sentinel* April 16, 1931, the same edition commenting editorially on the case wrote, "The swiftness of JUSTICE has added to its impressiveness."—(Emphasis, W.L.P.)

The editorial continued, "The only regrettable development in connection with the trial was the intrusion of certain Northern organizations with charges concerning the trial and demand concerning the criminals . . . Interference of this kind can serve no purpose other than to make it more difficult to stop lynchings in the South."

On the 5th of January 1932, Ruby Bates wrote to her sweetheart: "Those policemen made me tell a lie. . . . Those Negroes didn't touch me."

Who were "the criminals?" The Jackson County *Sentinel* was referring to the nine innocent Negro boys whom with inconceivable viciousness it had earlier labeled "beastly rapists," "brutal black fiends." It had made this reference with knowledge of these boys' innocence. It had lying[ly] written, "There was no demonstration" when its provocation of lynch hysteria had created the mob which marched around the court house with its band playing "There'll Be a Hot Time in the Old Town Tonight."

The letter of Ruby Bates has stripped the last shred of decency from those who control the courts of Alabama. It has disclosed the manner and the wherefore of legal lynch frame-ups.

The criminals were already murderers in their minds. They had legally lynched nine innocent boys. The electric current was only to add the official touch. Their hands were on the way to the switch. The hands of the murderers were stopped by those who had on so many occasions before (Pennsylvania, East Ohio, West Virginia, and Kentucky miners' strike, National Hunger March, Bonus March, etc.) shown such fearlessness in leading the struggle of the American workers. The murderous criminals are the bloody landlords and mill owners of Alabama and their tools, the scribblers on that slimy sheet, the Jackson County *Sentinel*.

The 13th, 14th and the 15th amendments in the United States Constitution supposedly guarantee certain "rights" to all. Particularly are these amendments supposed to apply to Negroes, yet, no official voice from the Republican Party spoke out to save these innocent black boys.

The Alabama Legal Code guarantees, they say, "A fair and impartial trial," yet no official voice from out the Democratic Party demanded this for these boys when the very "swiftness of justice" was obviously one of the most unjust factors associated with the case.

The silence of the Socialist Party leadership was of the same death-like character. The Negro reformists when they broke their silence, entered into a flood of abuse and condemnation against the Communists and in praise of those now shown to be the murderous criminals.

These elements without exception called for reverence and faith in the courts.

"The courts belong to the lynchers," said the Communist Party, calling for a mobilization of mass protest in defense of the innocent Negro boys. Only those from whose ranks these innocent victims come can save them. They are framed because the terrible conditions under which workers are now forced to live, breeding revolt, have caused unrest, have caused rebelliousness among the poverty-stricken, the most oppressed, and the Negroes must by terror if necessary, be kept from a struggle for their rights. These were the words of the International Labor Defense which rallied first to the cause of the Communists for mass action in behalf of the Scottsboro boys.

Now Ruby Bates, the star witness of the State of Alabama, against the Scottsboro boys, affirms the correctness of these statements and indicts the State. The State of Alabama has been indicted by the hundreds of lynch murders committed against known and unknown toiling Negroes and poor whites for which there has never been a conviction. It has been indicted by its murderous chain-gang system. Its own witness, Ruby Bates, only added a new indictment—"Those policemen made me tell a lie . . . Those Negroes didn't touch us."

The State of Alabama prepares the new legal lynch trial of the innocent Scottsboro boys and the Jackson County *Sentinel* now incites to mob lynching for fear the local lynching experience will prove ineffective, even after the implicit instructions handed down at the new trial decision. A wild wave of white Chauvinism (capitalist prejudice against Negroes) sweeps not only the South but the entire country.

Records of the International Labor Defense, Schomburg Center for Research in Black Culture, New York Public Library

Open letter

early March 1933

William L. Patterson, ILD Secretary

Dear Comrades:

Today the motion seeking to bring the trials of the nine innocent Scottsboro Boys in Birmingham, instead of Scottsboro, is being argued. Within two weeks, on March 20th, we expect the trials to begin.

Decisive steps must be taken to strengthen the defense. Your district must play a leading role. Scottsboro must be brought forward in your March 18th meetings. Thorough, painstaking preparations must be made for the March 20th demonstrations. Funds must be immediately raised for defense. We must send lawyers, technical workers, and a publicity representative into Scottsboro today! Victory or defeat hinges upon this, yet we are unable to act, for lack of funds.

The political significance of your help in solving this grave problem must not be underestimated. In a program sent to you January 19th we proposed that each I.L.D. member raise a minimum of one dollar for the SCOTTSBORO NEW TRIAL EMERGENCY FUND. Several districts report their adoption of this propos[al]. I and we are writing to urge you to do the same at once. As an emergency measure you cannot wait for the next DEC meeting, but must call in the DEC immediately, as well as every branch secretary, and place the situation before them.

In order to stimulate this activity, the NO has issued a one-hundred-penny-stamp sheet. The Stamps are to be pasted on letter[s], popularizing the Scottsboro Case and the I.L.D. The cost—one penny for each stamp—makes it within reach of ever[y] worker, providing the I.L.D. members reach sufficient number of workers. Urge the employed members to send in one dollar immediately and dispose of the stamps afterwards . . . the unemployed to give their time immediately to the sale of these stamps. Arrange for each branch secretary to collect the dollars within a specified time—say one week from the day of distribution—and rush the funds to the NO directly, retaining 30% for the District. We enclose proof of the stamp sheet and will send you as many as you can use. Please wire today how many you can use.

Recently, a fifty-five year old woman came to the NO. With tears in her eyes, she said, "I earn four dollars a week washing clothes and give three dollars for the Scottsboro Boys." Another unemployed worker walked some ten miles, from Bronx to Brooklyn, in order to contribute five cents, his carfare. These examples show the extents to which the workers are ready to make sacrifices for the Scottsboro Boys. We do not ask I.L.D. members to make such sacrifices. We must ask them to bring the message of Scottsboro, as a symbol of the oppression of the entire working-class, to their fellow workers. If this is done, energetically, then the workers will ride to the support of the defense struggle . . . then we will grow in numerical strength and financial problems will be, to a large extent, solved by the organized activity of our members.

We must have your answer—today!

Comradely yours,

William L. Patterson

NATIONAL SECRETARY

Records of the International Labor Defense, Schomburg Center for Research in Black Culture, New York Public Library

I.L.D. Statement.

March 1933

William L. Patterson

The Scottsboro Case and the I.L.D.

The International Labor Defense is an organization of defense based upon the principles of class struggle. It believes that "every class struggle is a political struggle," and its experience has been that every defense struggle at once takes on a political character.

Against the worker or poor farmer defendant at every point stand the united forces of the State. Whether the arrest be for picketing, as in the mining strikes in Kentucky, Pennsylvania, West Virginia and Ohio; in the farmers' milk strike in Rochester, New York, or the food strikes of the farmers in the Middle West; whether it be for participation in strike demonstrations like the New England textile strikes, the steel strikes, etc.; whether it be for engaging in a struggle against evictions, the shutting off of water, gas and electricity for non-payment; whether the arrest grows out of a demonstration of international solidarity against the deportation of alien workers or to develop unity and solidarity between Negro and white workers against lynch law justice, jim-crowism, or on the broader front of defense struggle, it makes little difference. If the worker, black or white, native or foreign-born, or those sympathizing with him, has sought to protect working class interests or lives, he finds, in the administration of the law, the hand of the State against him. The class struggle begun on the streets or in the shop is carried into the court room. The forces of working class defense rally the forces of capitalist "justice" and "democracy."

Capitalist "Justice"

Capitalist justice in theory is expressed in the beautiful democratic phrases contained in the constitutions of the capitalist

governments, in the high-sounding phrases by which the Judge
and the Prosecutor proclaim even-handed justice. The real class
essence of capitalist justice is exposed when an Angelo Herndon
is given 18 years at hard labor on the chain gang—his "crime"
was that he demanded bread and work for unemployed and
starving "forgotten" black and white toilers; when Mooney and
Billings, whose "crimes" were that they demanded for the working class the right to apply its right to organize, its right of free
speech, are given life imprisonment by a capitalist court; when
Sacco and Vanzetti are ruthlessly murdered to terrorize an awakening working class; when nine innocent youths of an oppressed
nation are railroaded to the electric chair to smash with terror
any striving of their people for national liberation. A clear analysis of these events helps to destroy the illusions of the impartiality of capitalist fair play.

The "Militant," organ in the United States of Mr. Trotzky,
who enjoys such prestige in the press of the capitalist world,
hurls a bouquet of slander and invective at the International
Labor Defense because of its utilization of the services of
Mr. Samuel S. Leibowitz, prominent attorney, in the Scottsboro
case. These "defenders" of principle tell us that this is proof that
the International Labor Defense has fallen upon evil days. "It
begins to look as though the International Labor Defense were
teetering on the brink of a piece of rotten and dangerous opportunism," we are informed.

To these saviors of the International Labor Defense, who
seek also to "save" the only political party of the working class by
betraying its fundamental principles, we answer, dear "friends",
we are afraid that the wish is father to the thought.

But our contempt for these friends does not relieve us of the
duty of dispelling the confusion they seek to create in the minds
of their followers. Their demagogy must be exposed as relentlessly
as we expose the democratic illusion about the impartially of justice which appears in the pages of the degenerate capitalist press
which so readily hires the services of their leader, Mr. Trotzky.

Lawyers and Mass Action

We are told by the "Militant" that the International Labor Defense, when it retains lawyers, swears them to silence "on all points where they disagree with it." But the "Militant" editors lie deliberately. The International Labor Defense imposes no such obligation, nor is it so simple as to regard this as possible.

International Labor Defense lawyers are engaged to serve it on the basis of their ability as "court-room technicians." The services of Mr. Walter Pollak, for example, were retained to argue the Scottsboro appeal in the Supreme Court because he was regarded as an expert in his particular field of law. The question of whether he agreed or disagreed with the basic policy of the International Labor Defense was not an issue. Certainly there was no talk of his agreeing "to interfere neither in word or deed with the International Labor Defense's conduct of the political struggle."

Mr. Pollak could not interfere with the mobilization of mass pressure by the International Labor Defense one way or another. Nor can any other attorney.

The opinions of Mr. Leibowitz on questions of politics and economics are not considered by the International Labor Defense. His attitude in the court room is, however. Were he to hesitate "to speak and compel the court to adhere to the rules of court procedure formulated by the government itself, but which were systematically violated by the agents of the court" when workers and their sympathizers were on trial, his connections with the International Labor Defense would be severed.

Leibowitz's Task

Mr. Leibowitz is carrying out the line of the International Labor Defense in the court room in this particular case. This was the condition imposed upon him. He was not asked to nor could he engage in the political defense of the accused, but his legal defense of the accused is political. It is not a condition that he agree with the entire viewpoints of the International Labor Defense. But he has openly declared in the court room, "If it were not for the International Labor Defense these nine boys would now be dead."

Mr. Leibowitz is asked to fight the Scottsboro frame-up from the legal point of view, to take advantage of every contradiction in the bosses' law and Mr. Leibowitz is satisfactorily carrying out this task. Our own task is to draw the correct political conclusions from the attempts of Mr. Thomas E. Knight, Jr., representative of the State, to deny to Negroes their constitutional rights and to murder innocent boys. Our own task is to awaken the working class.

Our dubious friends of the "Militant" demand a united front with members of the bar. So, gentlemen, this is your conception of the "Leninist tactic of the united front" on the field of working class defense struggles. We contemptuously reject your viewpoint. It was not in this sense, take note, that Lenin ever said that the lawyer was "the instrument, the tool of the class which employs him." You say: "Only if the relationship is on such basis (united front with the lawyer-W.L.P.) can the International Labor Defense relate a good legal fight to the fundamental and essential political fight. The International Labor Defense does not "relate" the one to the other. With the International Labor Defense these struggles remain inseparably related.

Gentlemen, it is not the lawyer who represents the working class in the capitalist courts. We are the representatives of the working class, as is also the defendant. The lawyer is not a revolutionist, nor does the sale or contribution of his services to a revolutionary organization make him one. It is, of course, not unnatural that you should think in terms of the purchased "revolutionist." The sale of so much of Mr. Trotzky's "revolutionary" writing to the capitalist press undoubtedly has been a factor in leading you to this "mistake."

It is the worker defendant who uses the court as his forum. It is he who introduces the social and economic questions so vital to an exposure of the court as the weapon of class rule. It is not the lawyer who politicizes the defense struggles led by the International Labor Defense, but his legal defense which is politicized by the International Labor Defense. Mr. Leibowitz under the direction of the International Labor Defense, is fighting for the constitutional rights of the Negroes and the white workers as well. Thus he is helping to politicize the Scottsboro case.

Where Verdicts Are Rendered

The courtrooms of the working class are the streets. It is in the streets that they must pass their verdict of innocence on the class war victim. When they in sufficient numbers have done this, that verdict will be reflected by a judge and jury in capitalist courts. That Mr. Pollak did or did not express any disagreement with the policy of the International Labor Defense did not influence the Supreme Court in the reversal of the lynch verdict of Alabama. The Scottsboro boys were saved by mass pressure. The campaign of the International Labor Defense balanced the scales in favor of the boys. The united voice of an outraged working class was too loud to ignore.

Incidentally, the ruling class of the South threatens Mr. Leibowitz with death because in the court room his fight is tearing at the basis of their system. Mr. Leibowitz's conduct has strengthened the basis of struggle for the International Labor Defense. He has exposed the hypocrisy of capitalist law. The danger to the lives of the boys lies in the failure of the entire labor movement to mobilize around their defense. What part have the gentlemen of the "Militant" played in this mobilization?

The determining factor in the class struggle in the capitalist courts, or elsewhere, is the relation of class forces. That is why success rests with the working class defendant only where the mobilization of the working class and its sympathizers around him is raised to an overwhelming[ly] high political level. The center of support must be shifted from reliance upon mass pressure.

Basic International Labor Defense Policy

The International Labor Defense believes that only mass pressure can bring about the release of a class war prisoner; that pressure must be supplemented by legal defense. The legal defense must be of the mot expert character. Every legal technicality must be used. The more far-reaching the knowledge of the lawyer retained by the International Labor Defense, the more easily and effectively can the worker be shown that the guarantees of justice extended him by the ruling class are meaningless.

Mr. Leibowitz has this expert knowledge. Every report coming out of the Decatur court house shows him in the forefront along the line of the International Labor Defense of the legal battle for every right supposedly guaranteed the innocent defendants, by State and Federal Constitutions. He has brought out the class character of this case with the utmost clarity because he followed the International Labor Defense line.

Mass Pressure Only Guarantee

Mass pressure by the American working class, mobilized to that point where the ruling class recognizes its potential force, is the only guarantee of safety for the Scottsboro boys. This mobilization does not rest alone in the hands of the International Labor Defense. It rests in the hands of the entire leadership of the American working class. This mobilization can be realized only to the extent that the American working class is made to recognize that the struggle against the system of national oppression, and for the democratic rights of the Negro masses, is a part and parcel of the struggle for the democratic rights of the working class as a whole.

In the Scottsboro case, the International Labor Defense has achieved its greatest success defending the rights of members of an oppressed nation. It has, therefore, achieved its greatest success in the defense of the democratic rights of the working class of America as a whole. It has advanced this defense to a high political level under Lenin's slogans repudiated by the righteous "defenders of principles" who control the "Militant." Without a relentless united struggle for equal rights for Negroes, white workers cannot realize complete democracy. Without the right to self-determination, the toiling Negro masses cannot secure equal rights.

Onward to mass mobilization of the American working class in defense of the Scottsboro boys of Tom Mooney and all class war prisoners! An end to capitalist justice!

William Patterson in Stirring Call for Scottsboro Unity
Harlem Address Stresses the Fight Against Local Lynchers
Daily Worker

April 19, 1933

NEW YORK. Two thousand workers, Negro and white, roared their approval time after time as William Patterson, National Secretary of the International Labor Defense, ripped the mask from misleaders who are shouting "united front" in the Scottsboro case. Patterson's speech climaxed the Scottsboro protest meeting that filled the Abyssinian Nation Church in Harlem, Monday night.

The I.L.D. national security followed a list of speakers that included Walter White of the N.A.A.C.P., Heywood Broun, Reader of the National Urban League, Benjamin J. Davis, Jr., attorney with John Geer in the Angelo Herndon case, Mrs. Joyce Bushell from the Harlem Democratic organization, William Davis, owner of the Amsterdam News and others.

"I want to touch upon two points, unity and concrete action to save the Scottsboro Boys. First however, I am going to tell you facts and let you draw your own conclusion," Patterson said in opening his tempestuous speech.

Roosevelt - Enslaver of Haiti

"The man in the White House is the man who drafted the constitution that is holding the people of Haiti in slavery." (The

audience interrupted with stamping of feet and cheers and excla-
mations of 'that's right"—he continued.)

"You have heard a lot about the united front tonight. We want
a united front and we're going to have [the] kind of united front
that will save the Scottsboro Boys (cheers). Mayor O'Brian and
Tammany Hall are trying to make a political football out of the
misery of the Negro people for 350 years.

"Tonight speakers have told you that 5,000 Negroes have
been lynched since the Civil War. Yes there have been 5,000 such
lynchings and the Republican and Democratic Parties have done
nothing about it. You've got to learn how to fight every inch of
the way—against every act of national oppression. Tonight they
have spoken to you about the flag and the home of the free, right
on this platform. They told you here tonight that there was
no discrimination in Harlem. What about that butchers shop,
Harlem hospital? What about the extra rents you have to pay?
What about the restaurants and hotels right in Harlem that you
can't enter? These are the Scottsboros, you are not in Alabama.
(cheering) These must be fought if the Scottsboro Boys are to be
saved. Those [who] are trying to divert the growing unity of the
Negro people are playing with dynamite and we're letting them
know it now (cheering).

"No More Betrayals!"

"I tell you Mr. Davis (owner of the Amsterdam News)—for two
years the I.L.D. has led the struggle for the nine innocent
Scottsboro Boys. Oppression of the Negro people, of the white
workers, Jim-crowism, lynching, all these must be brought into
the Scottsboro case because the I.L.D. is not going to form a
united front with the lynchers of America (shouts of no-no).
Only the I.L.D. is authorized to collect funds for the Scottsboro
case. Those who are collecting money [Davis is collecting funds
for a "march" on Washington that has already dwindled down in
his statements from 50,000 to a group of representative citizens
of Harlem] better see that it gets into the right hands, not to the

I.L.D. but to these 2000 channels or they will have to answer, workers and all the Negro and white workers of New York. (Right, right, cheers).

"I know that you (the Negro people and white workers) are tired of betrayals. I know you want to fight. We don't want to fight anyone claiming to be in the fight for these boys but we know how to fight. (Thunderous ovation). If any of you get out of line, we will whip you back into line. (cheers)

"Thousands will March"

"Thousands of Negro and white workers are going to march on Washington on April 28. Recruiting stations will be opened in Harlem and as far west as Chicago. We're going there not to beg but to demand. (cheers) We are presenting a bill to enforce the 13th, 14th, and 16th amendments to the constitution. We want those demands enforced and we are going to have them enforced. These are what our forefathers slaved for and our fathers fought for.

"Mr. Reade says that they could have freed the Scottsboro Boys and taken the wind out of our sails. This isn't so. This wind in our sails is that of slavery and we are going to blow it out with wind of freedom for the Negro nation in America. I have to conclude now (Shouts of 'Keep on, we'll sit here, all night, give him more time'). No comrades it isn't time. It is other work I have yet to do today. If it were only time, I would stay here all night."

The audience rose in tribute when Mother Patterson entered the meeting. She spoke briefly as follows: "I am not well. My mind is in the balance. You mothers know how heavy my load is. I want you to support the I.L.D. and free my boy and those other children." The audience rose in a tribute. A collection of over $120 was taken for the Scottsboro defense.

Benjamin Davis received an ovation when he said, "The fight for Angelo Herndon, is inseparable from the fight of the Scottsboro Boys, Tom Mooney, the fight of the Negro people and white workers for freedom.

Frank Palmer, representing the American Civil Liberties Union proposed that the Free Tom Mooney meeting at Bronx Coliseum Thursday, April 27 be changed into a Scottsboro-Mooney mass meet. Wm. Patterson nodded his head in agreement and the audience cheered.

Democratic Demagogy

Mrs. Bushnell was interrupted in her praise of President Roosevelt by a shout of "No democratic propaganda speak of Scottsboro or shut up." The audience cheered this demand and she closed her remarks among which was the hypocritical statement that "there is no discrimination in the 21 A.D. I would not stand for it. I am your co-leader for 10 years and know your problems." Urban Klein, I. L.D. attorney, and member of the Scottsboro staff, told how not only one lawyer had served without pay but that more of them had done that for the past two years. He called for clear support of the I.L.D. The audience cheered him. Prof. Joshua Kunitz gave an eyewitness' report of the Decatur trial. Two telegrams were sent to President Roosevelt and Gov. Miller of Alabama demanding freedom of the boys and equal political, social and economic rights of Negroes.

Walter White merely said that the N.A.A.C.P. members could give money to either the I.L.D. or their own organization and explained how the N.A.A.C.P. had arranged to account to the I.L.D. He received a lukewarm reception and stated twice, "I am not here to defend the National Association. It stands on its record." The audience showed their appraisal of that record by their silence.

Heywood Broun admitted he was coming into the fight late. He said that "some people are avoiding the United Front because they are afraid of being stepped on We can all unite to save these boys." Rev. Powell presided as chairman.

Monitoring the Case

International Labor Defense attorney *Joseph R Brodsky, in April 1933, filed a motion with Judge Horton for a new trial for Haywood Patterson on the grounds that the conviction was against the weight of the evidence. The Scottsboro defendants, on April 28, protested ill-treatment in Jefferson County Jail, Birmingham, with a hunger strike. On May 5, on a mass Scottsboro march to Washington, D.C., black and white protesters carried a petition signed by 200,000 people that demanded freedom for the "Scottsboro Nine." On May 28, Ruby Bates joined a delegation to the White House headed by William Patterson. Vice-President John N. Garner met with the delegation. In early June, Judge Horton ordered two of the youths under sixteen years of age transferred to the Juvenile Court. Those youths were Eugene Williams and Roy Wright.*

On June 22, Judge Horton granted the motion for a new trial for Haywood Patterson and set aside the conviction with a lengthy opinion reviewing the case and concluding that the conviction was unjustified by the evidence. Horton believed that Victoria Price had lied on the witness stand.

Horton's decision elicited an international response from International Red Aid, the international parent body for the ILD.

Fond 515, Files of the Communist Party of the United States in the Comintern Archives

Telegram from International Red Aid to ILD, Moscow, USSR, to International Labor Defense, New York

Executive committee International Red Aid greets New Trial Patterson as result mass effort organized by International Labor Defense stop executive committee confident I.L.D. will increase activity for release of Scottsboro boys Mooney Billings all other political prisoners and support relief of victims German fascist terror stop executive committee believes I.L.D. will broaden its base by drawing into its ranks new negro and white workers and give added proof correctness of policy.

Again giving voice to the Scottsboro parents, Communists published an open letter from Claude Patterson, Haywood Patterson's father.

Records of the International Labor Defense, Schomburg Center for Research in Black Culture, New York Public Library

"My Son Was Convicted Because He Is Black," Writes Father of Haywood Patterson

Open Letter from Claude Patterson (Haywood Patterson's father)

July 1, 1933

I am the father of Haywood Patterson and quite naturally interested in his case down in Alabama and you have recently published editorials in which you exposed the wish that the International Labor Defense should withdraw from all connection with this case.

I would appreciate giving you and the public through your valuable paper a short history of this case with unpublished facts that will aid and clarify many things and to correct erroneous impressions about this case.

When this trouble started and the nine boys were arrested at Scottsboro, they had made no preparation for trial, no witnesses, no employed attorney and were forced into trial unprepared; convicted by a combination of circumstances and the public greatly misled by the false testimony introduced in that trial.

The Arrest

At that time the trouble occurred, a crew of white boys attacked a number of colored boys, threw rocks at them and provoked a fight in a flat car on a long train of about 50 cars in a row; this fight was in flat car number four counting from the rear end of the train and the two women were in flat five, one car ahead of the fight.

When the fight was over and the white boys jumped off except one man named Gilley. He was trying to swing off but he was about to be killed under the car wheels and Haywood Patterson. Andy Wright and Charley Weems pulled him back up on the train and let him remain there.

When the train reached Paint Rock, Alabama, an order had been made to arrest all the Negroes on the train because of the fight.

After they were taken to Scottsboro, the report spread that they had been accused of assaulting the two white women who were in the car in front of where this fight occurred. This report only tried to be started and the Hunterville Times and the Jackson County Sentinel would do the rest as newspaper corresponders and from those the news was carried about how the white boys saw the alleged crime, knew all about it and witnessed it.

No [worse] batch of lies was ever written or penned by the hand of man, than the batch of lies sent out from Scottsboro about these innocent boys and if you will bear with me, I will tell you about it.

In order to make the women swear lies and stick to it they were both locked up in the same jail with the white boys and colored boys in separate cells, but why put the women in jail? Put in there to hold them and make them tell lies, so Randy Bates has said.

Why put those seven white boys in jail? Put them in jail to make them swear lies, so Lester Carter says, but not one of the white boys ever testified against my son, Haywood Patterson, in Scottsboro, and all the white boys were released and not one of them ever testified in any case against Haywood Patterson. Did they see a crime committed? No, sir. Well, why were they kept in jail at Scottsboro?

They told my son and these other boys that it was a frame-up lie and they were not going to testify to such a batch of lies as that was, and they did not testify to it. Not one of the white boys ever took the witness stand against my boy.

When the trial came on, two witnesses, Victoria Price and Ruby Bates testified against all these nine boys and they were convicts, and while that mock trial was going on, the International Labor Defense had a man from New York sitting in the audience who reported that it was the greatest mock trial ever held in the State of Alabama. This case was held when I was afraid to go to Scottsboro for fear of mob violence and I employed George W. Chamlee, attorney, of Chattanooga, Tenn., to represent my son as he had been my lawyer before that time. Just at that time, Mr. Brodsky of the International Labor Defense, and its chief counsel from New York came to Chattanooga, and said he would help me pay the expenses of this case on an appeal, and the appeal was taken and a new trial granted in the Supreme Court at Washington and the expenses of printing that record was about $1,500 alone.

If it had not been for the International Labor Defense coming to our assistance quickly, in time to file a motion for a new trial and set up a real defense, the boys would have all been killed, although they were all innocent.

In one of your editorials, you suggested that all we needed was some good Southern attorneys, like Mr. Roddy and Mr. Moody and the boys would have a chance to be acquitted.

Well, Judge Hawkins had them while the trial in his court was on and when the State's Attorney got up and shook his finger in the faces of these boys, denounced them, demanded the death penalty for them, no attorney got up and offered one word of argument or any summation, on behalf of these nine boys, and then a second attorney for the state demanded the death penalty and Mr. Roddy and Mr. Moody declined to argue the cases.

"We Had a Trial Recently"

We had a trial at Decatur recently and the State had one star witness, Victoria Price an underworld character, who had been convicted in the courts of Huntsville for vagrancy, lewdness and violating the prohibition law; she had broken up the family of Jack Tiller, and Tiller's wife had to take her children and leave him; this woman swore she spent the night at Mrs. Callie Broochie's boarding house on 7th St. in Chattanooga, while Ruby Bates, Lester Carter and E.L. Lewis and Dallas Ramsay all swore she spent the night in the woods on the bank of Chattanooga creek. On her testimony, practically alone with no witness to the facts, and her evidence contradicted by five colored boys, in addition to other impeaching items against her, a death penalty was pronounced upon my son.

The big lie [was] that Ruby Bates had been bribed. Who bribed her? When and where was she bribed? She has been trying to join the defendants from the first day she was put in jail in Scottsboro. Who bribed Lester Carter? Where did he get this bribe? Why was Carter and Gilley not used on the trial in Scottsboro, if they knew anything material?

"My Boy Saved Gilley"

My boy pulled Gilley up on the train to keep him from being killed, while attempting to jump off. Was Gilley afraid of him then? Sure not.

Dr. Bridges testified that two hours after Victoria Price was arrested and put in jail, he examined her, that she was not even nervous, hysterical, or that there were any serious hurts, only a few scratches, and no injury, and his testimony proved no crime was committed.

Why did the jury convict Haywood Patterson in Alabama when he is absolutely innocent? Because it was a white woman accusing a Negro boy. If it had been a Negro woman accusing a white boy, he would never have been indicted, or if it had been two Negro girls accusing seven white boys and one Negro woman came up confessing her lies, as Ruby Bates has done, that would have been the end of this litigation.

Haywood Patterson was convicted because he is black. No other reason, no other excuse, no other cause, none wanted, entirely innocent.

On November 20, 1933 Haywood Patterson went on trial for the third time, this time before Judge William Washington Callahan, at Decatur. Three days later, the defense challenged the authenticity of seven African American names placed on the jury roll, charging forgery. On December 1, Haywood Patterson was convicted for the third time and again the death sentence was imposed. Clarence Norris was put on trial immediately afterwards and then convicted and similarly sentenced a week later. It was Norris's second trial, his first, like that of the others, having been at Scottsboro. Samuel Liebowitz, Joseph R. Brodsky, and George W. Chamlee of Chattanooga represented both defendants.

William Patterson immediately responded to these developments.

Records of the International Labor Defense, Schomburg Center for Research in Black Culture, New York Public Library

"Scottsboro Protest Must Grow"

Labor Defender

February 1934

William L. Patterson

The second Decatur trial was a revelation to tens of thousands of white and Negro workers. The class character of American courts was never made more clear. There was no attempt to disguise the class role of the judge and the prosecutor. The method of these agents of the ruling class making use of the jury as an instrument with which to carry out their murderous attack, and behind which to hide the real face of ruling class justice had the full glare of a search light thrown upon it. All who cared to see could see the picture of the bourgeois class justice in action without its mask.

The second Decatur trial of the innocent Scottsboro boys has greatly strengthened the influence and prestige of the I.L.D. among the masses. Judge Callahan made no effort to hide behind gestures of liberalism. He was no James E. Horton. He came forward with brazen viciousness as a propagandist of the landlords and bankers whose most effective slogan is "Divide and Rule." He came forward to uphold the glory of "white supremacy."

He sought to destroy all sympathy for the Negro people. He sought to smash the basis for their unity with the ever growing number of white worker victims of the white ruling class fascist lynch terror. There was no crime, no act of depravity too low to be placed at the door of the Negro people. He reaffirmed the decision of the chief justice Taney of the U. S. Supreme Court in 1857 "The Black Man Has No Rights which a White Man is bound to Respect." The innocence of these Negro boys made it necessary to be extremely vicious.

But Judge Callahan, the ruling class propagandist, has failed to smash the growing solidarity of the Negro and white masses. Capitalist justice is everywhere showing its murderous hand. Growing fascist terror merged with lynch violence is opening the eyes of the white workers to the need of solidarity in struggle. White workers have been murdered in California cotton fields because they demanded a living wage, in Mexico's coal fields because they refused to labor at starvation wages, in Pennsylvania's steel mills, in the textile mills of the New England mill barons, and behind each murderous attack stand the forces who seek to divide that they may continue to rule.

Judge Callahan has strikingly proven the correctness of the position of the International Labor Defense. The courts are one of the strongest weapons of the ruling class.

Scottsboro has raised the question of international working class solidarity to its highest level.

It is linking Tom Mooney, Angelo Herndon, the Mexican Boys of Brighton Colo,. the Cuban workers of Tampa, Fla. and the oppressed Negro masses inseparably together.

The growing solidarity of the oppressed masses native and foreign born, white and black, unemployed and employed, around the ever increasing defense battles, and the concessions they have gained, prove that the International Labor Defense is the only guarantee for success in the struggle for the freedom of our class war prisoners.

In April 1934 black Communist Benjamin J. Davis, Jr., a graduate of Harvard Law School, wrote Samuel Liebowitz a letter reporting on mistreatment of the Scottsboro defendants in jail. Liebowitz protested the mistreatment to Alabama authorities.

Records of the International Labor Defense, Schomburg Center for Research in Black Culture, New York Public Library

The Scottsboro Boys

Letter from Ben Davis to Samuel Liebowitz

April 1934

The last time I visited the Scottsboro boys in Jefferson County jail, I carried them a carton of cigarettes, matches and stamps. Following the usual custom, I expected the packages to be examined and returned to me for distribution as I interviewed them. But this time Deputy Warden Rogers, refused to permit me to deliver them. He took the packages and marked on them for "The Scottsboro Niggers." This was done plainly and conspicuously so that I might be intimidated into understanding the treatment accorded to all "niggers" whether they were lawyers or prisoners.

Then Warden Rogers, as he led me to the cells for interview stated he "didn't know what had gotten into them Scottsboro niggers. They're the worse bunch of niggers he ever saw. Always raising hell when they get the best treatment possible."

But the seven Scottsboro boys in Jefferson County jail tell a different story about the "best treatment possible." And Wright was confined in solitary for more than 3 weeks because he refused to go "outside in the snow and sleet to catch a death cold." This was at the request of Warden Dan Rogers. Then Montgomery was placed in solitary because he kicked against the starvation portion put on his food plate. Warden Rogers considered this "the best treatment possible."

Warden Rogers asked one of the boys "who is that nigger lawyer who came in here, a son of a bitch. I wish I could catch him sitting in the court house here. I'd hang him." He also told the boys, that "as long as that nigger lawyer keeps coming down here smelling your heads you're going to stay in solitary. You'd better keep him away."

Once Warden Rogers brandished his pistol on one of the boys threatening to kill him. As the boy pleaded for his life, Rogers belched, "I ought to kill you now, they're going to kill you anyway, just like they're going to burn Patterson and Norris."

The boys all are mortally afraid that Warden Rogers will someday shoot them down in cold blood. At every opportunity he curses them, browbeats them and attempts to provoke them into defending themselves in order that he might murder them for "resisting an officer of the law." He plants stool pigeons in their cells. These stool pigeons provoke fights which result in the boys being thrown into solitary while the stool pigeons are never punished. Then he boasts to the boys that "I'll always believe my stool pigeons un preference to you niggers."

A stool pigeon framed one of the boys a month ago by claiming he had stolen 50 cents from him. This boy has been in solitary now for more than five weeks without change of clothes or a bath. This same torturer Rogers also claims that the boy has a razor in his possession, and threatens to keep him in solitary until the razor is delivered up. The truth is that this boy has never had a razor in his possession and obviously has no way of obtaining one even to secure his release from solitary.

Warden Rogers has repeatedly informed the boys that as long as people come to see them they will stay in solitary. Recently when Myra Page, well known writer, visited them, Warden Rogers called her a white whore and yelled "as long as white whores come down here to see you, we're not going to let you out."

In spite of all the concentrated terror and brutality unleashed upon them recently, the boys understand clearly that it is not accidental or spontaneous. As they said to me, "We know they're trying to divide us, but they can't. They're trying to force us to take the NAACP, but we don't want it. Warden Rogers is trying to find an excuse to kill us in jail, but we know and we're going to stick together and watch him." These 7 innocent boys in Jefferson County jail still have confidence in the ILD and the fighting unity of the negro and white workers who alone can save them. They are daily realizing that the sadistic tortures of Warden Rogers are a part of the same bloody system which framed them 3 years ago, and they look hopefully to the same ILD, the same world protest to save them from the new intensified campaign of terror against them.

Records of the International Labor Defense, Schomburg Center for Research in Black Culture, New York Public Library

ILD Telegram to Alabama Supreme Court APRIL 11, 1934
Copies to: Governor B.M. Miller
State Supreme Court, Ala.
Warden, Kilby Prison, Montgomery, Ala.

PROTEST REFUSAL PERMISSION DAVIS ILD ATTORNEY SEE PATTERSON NORRIS DEMAND IMMEDIATE RESCINDING THIS ILLEGAL ORDER IMMEDIATE UNCONDITIONAL RELEASE OF ALL THE SCOTTSBORO BOYS WHO HAVE BEEN PROVEN INNOCENT IN YOUR COURTS STOP ROUSING PROTEST THROUGHOUT COUNTRY AGAINST THIS ACTION AND AGAINST TORTURE OF SEVEN BOYS IN THE JEFFERSON COUNTY JAIL

WILLIAM L PATTERSON

NATIONAL SECRETARY

INTERNATIONAL LABOR DEFENSE

On May 13, five Scottsboro mothers, accompanied by Ruby Bates, called at the White House on Mother's Day. President Franklin Roosevelt was out. Almost two weeks later, appeals in both cases were argued in the Alabama Supreme Court by Samuel S. Liebowitz and Osmond K. Fraenkel. The ILD, on June 23, mailed the president a complete documented statement on the case, demanding his intervention. Five days later, the Alabama Supreme Court affirmed the convictions.

In October 1934, Samuel S. Liebowitz formed the American Scottsboro Committee (ASC). On January 7, 1935, the United States Supreme Court granted petitions for review of the convictions of Patterson and Norris. From February 15 to 18, appeals were argued by Samuel Liebowitz, retained by the American Scottsboro Committee, and Walter H. Pollak and Osmond Fraenkel, retained by the International Labor Defense. The Supreme Court, on April 1, reversed the convictions of both defendants on the ground that African Americans were excluded from the panel of grand and petit jurors which indicted and tried them.

Alabama prepared for more prosecution. On May 1, new warrants were sworn out by Victoria Price, the only complaining witness since the withdrawal of Ruby Bates. The grand jury at Scottsboro, on November 13, returned new indictments for rape against all the defendants, including the two transferred to Juvenile Court. One black citizen, Creed Conyer, sat on the grand jury for the first time in the memory of any resident of Alabama. A two-thirds vote was sufficient to return the indictment.

In December 1935 the ASC was dissolved and the Scottsboro Defense Committee (SDC) was formed, composed of all groups cooperating in the defense. The SDC was made up of representatives of the International Labor Defense, the National Association for the Advancement of Colored People, the American Civil Liberties Union, the Methodist Federation for Social Service, the League for Industrial Democracy, and the Church League for Industrial Democracy (Episcopal). The Scottsboro Defense Committee took over the legal defense, while the ILD continued its public campaign for the freedom of the nine.

Early in January 1936 the Scottsboro defendants, excluding the two juveniles, were arraigned and pled not guilty. Judge Callahan rejected petitions for removal to the United States District Court. On January 20, Liebowitz, C. L. Watts, of Huntsville, Alabama, and George W. Chamlee, conducted Patterson's defense. Three days later Haywood Patterson was convicted for the fourth time. Judge Callahan sentenced him to seventy-five years in prison. The nine defendants, on January 24, were on the way back to Birmingham jail. An incident occurred in the automobile of Sheriff J. Street Sandlin, of Decatur. Ozie Powell slashed a deputy; Sandlin shot Powell.

Records of the International Labor Defense, Schomburg Center for Research in Black Culture, New York Public Library

Alabama Lynchers Strive to Hide Facts Of Murderous Attack on Scottsboro Boys

January 30, 1936

Ben Davis

The Alabama sheriffs who murderously attacked Ozie Powell, one of the Scottsboro Boys, are already attempting to hide their bloody hands behind a tissue of conflicting lies.

The tell-tale operating table where young Powell was placed after reaching Birmingham reveals that all of the contradictory stories given by the same three officers implicated in the lynch attempts are pure fabrications.

Sheriff Sandlin, who claimed he was riding in the front seat with Deputy Sheriff Blaylock, allegedly "slashed by Powell," stated, "I shot Powell in the face when he slashed a deputy and tried to escape." Powell and two other of the boys handcuffed together were occupying the back seat.

Earlier reports were that Blaylock himself had done the shooting. THE EAR, AND ABOUT AN INCH lips of State Highway Patrolman J.T. Bryant, who was in the car behind with Haywood Patterson and two other boys. He declared, "In the general scuffle to get my gun back it went off and shot Powell in the head."

From Operating Room

But the story from the operating room is that the WOUNDS WERE HIGH ON THE HEAD, BEHIND THE EAR, AND ABOUT AN INCH APART. OZIE POWELL WAS SHOT FROM THE BACK-NOT ONCE, BUT TWICE. The surgeon's examination showed that there were two wounds and both had been caused by bullets.

The lie that young Powell "tried to escape" reeks of Hitler Germany and Fascist Italy. The lad was handcuffed to two other Scottsboro boys seated inside a car locked from the inside, with two police bloodhounds inside the same car itching to use their guns. How anyone could believe that any sort of escape could even be attempted under these conditions is beyond the imagination of sane human beings!

At the time the attempted lynching occurred, the car was near Cullman, Ala., an all-white town of 3,500 inhabitants. No Negro is permitted to live [t]here and a large, plainly legible sign in the town reads: "Nigger, don't let the sun set on your head in this town."

It is ridiculous to believe that the three Scottsboro boys heavily handcuffed would seek to escape into a place where they would be lynched upon sight!

What could be clearer than the fact that this "tried to escape" pretext is a part of the same "rape" frame-up which has kept these boys in the torture chambers of Alabama for the last five years!

The Southern lynch class spreads the vicious propaganda that Negroes are "brutes, savages, and beasts" fit only for lynching, discrimination, starvation, and oppression.

But let us see who are the "brutes, savages, and beasts!"

Although Powell was in an almost dying condition, with a bullet an inch deep in his brain and with blood pouring from his head and face, he was taken FIRST TO THE BIRMINGHAM JAIL and NOT for medical treatment. People treat dogs better than this!

Dumped Out of Car

Suffering intense agony, the wounded boy could not get out of the automobile. Still handcuffed to the two other boys he was brutally dumped out of the car on the ground. Sheriff Sandlin barked, "Get up." Powell moaned, "Oh, Lord, I can't."

The "brutes, savages and beasts" are the police lynch agents of the Southern ruling class, who would murder the nine innocent Scottsboro boys!

The lies which the Alabama officials and sheriffs are spewing to cover this dastardly crime, come from the same source that has for five years tried to send these same boys to their death through legal lynching. They grow out of the desperation of the ruling class which has been three times prevented from "killing its prey" by a world wide mass movement. They grow out of desperation of an oppressing class which shakes with fear and rage at the growing unity of Negro and white workers, sharecroppers, liberals and professionals.

Free Scottsboro Boys

But that ruling class will forever strike back—and each time will be more desperate and fiercer than the last.

That is why the Negro people and all fair-minded people must form closer bonds of unity, and must fight harder to free the Scottsboro boys, the Negro people—and against budding fascism.

That is why the National Negro Congress must thunder the demand: "The Scottsboro boys shall not die."

That is why the broadest and most immediate support must be given to the Scottsboro Defense Committee.

A compromise between Alabama and the defense was reached in July 1937. Authorities sentenced Ozie Powell, who pled guilty to the charge of assault with intent to murder, to twenty years in prison. However, the original rape charge against Powell and the four others was dropped. The state of Alabama announced the release of Roy Wright, Olen Montgomery, Eugene Williams, and Willie Roberson. Authorities returned the others to prison.

It was African American Communist Benjamin Davis who took up the task in the second half of the thirties of following through on the Party's participation in the Scottsboro case.

"Two Scottsboro Mothers Urge Fight for Boys"

Daily Worker

July 30, 1937

Ben Davis

Two Scottsboro mothers arrived in New York at the Pennsylvania station yesterday afternoon—their faces beaming with a joy unknown to them since their sons were framed in Scottsboro, Ala., more than six years ago.

The mothers, Mrs. Ada Wright, mother of Roy and Andy, and Mrs. Viola Montgomery, mother of Olen, came to the city to see their two boys for the first time since they were freed. The Negro youths Roy and Olen, along with Willie Roberson and Eugene Williams, have been in New York since they were released last Saturday.

Mrs. Wright and Mrs. Montgomery came from their homes respectively in Chattanooga, Tenn., and Atlanta, Ga. Spectators crowded around them at the station tendering their congratulation[s]. Red caps eagerly pledged a "fight to the end."

Happy at Freedom

Her dark brown face wreathed in smiles, Mrs. Wright, who has toured Europe and America in the interest of the nine Negro boys said:

"I'm so sorry I hardly know what to say."

But deep in her heart, sorrow was mingled with happiness. Far more graphically than any person alive today Mrs. Wright symbolizes the tragi-comedy of the internationally famous case. While her younger son Roy is free, her first-born son Andy, the favorite of her large family, is still imprisoned under a 99-year sentence in Alabama.

Mrs. Montgomery, who with her 12-year old daughter, Mary Alice, arrived a few minutes after Mrs. Wright, hasn't seen her son in two years.

Tears in Eyes

"Although I have not seen him. I feel almost as happy just knowing he is out of that awful dungeon," Mrs. Montgomery stated her eyes filling with tears.

"We can't be too thankful to the Scottsboro Defense Committee, the International Labor Defense, and Mr. Leibowitz for this great victory. We feel that all those, Negro and white, who helped make this victory possible are helping the fight for our race," the two women said.

"We shall always have a special place in our hearts for the I.L.D., Mr. Joe Brodsky and the Communist Party, too, for they have stuck by us from the beginning when our boys were first sentenced to die. Through thick and thin they have been with us," stated Mrs. Montgomery.

"I visited the boys in prison about a month ago. Haywood Patterson who always was a good-looking boy, didn't look well. He looked sick. It just means that we've got to hurry and get the other five boys out, before they rot in jail," Mrs. Wright continued.

Patterson, under a 75-year sentence, recently underwent an operation in prison for an infected knee. Considered the "leader" of the boys, he has been tortured more regularly and brutally than any of the rest.

Boys Help Home

Herself a domestic worker and unemployed for more than a year, Mrs. Wright explained that Roy, even while in jail, would "deny himself things" to send a dollar home. Although Andy is the "sweetest" she went on, Roy has a sense of responsibility "way beyond his age, just like an old man."

"When I first heard the news I felt like crying, thinking how long my boy had been in jail, his eye-sight nearly failing him from the way the jailers treated him. Even now I tremble when I think how close he came to death. They nearly lynched all the boys in 1931 when they first arrested them. Even after that they kept on sentencing them to die," Mrs. Montgomery said.

"I didn't want to cry when I got the news about the boys being free, because I knew everyone else would cry. But that night, I couldn't help it—I cried all night. This is a real victory for Negroes, especially in the South.

"As for the I.L.D., nobody will ever take that organization away from me. The freedom of the boys shows what the unity of

Negro and white can do. It's going to free the other boys as sure as I'm alive."

Appearing much thinner than when she was in New York three years ago, Mrs. Montgomery explained:

"I've lost considerable weight in the long fight for the boys. But I'll pick it up now that Olen in free. And I won't stop fighting till all of them are free."

"Scottsboro Appeal Filed in Alabama by Defense Committee"

Daily Worker

August 6, 1937

Ben Davis

Definite legal steps toward the freedom of the five imprisoned Scottsboro boys began yesterday when appeals from their recent convictions were dispatched to the Alabama Circuit Courts, the Scottsboro Defense Committee announced late yesterday afternoon. The appeals will be considered filed when they reach the Alabama tribunal today.

Osmond K. Fraenkel, noted constitutional attorney, retained by the Committee, sent the appeals yesterday. They will ask for a new trial in the following cases: Andy Wright sentenced to 99 years; Clarence Norris, sentenced to death; Charlie Weems, sentenced to 75 years; and Haywood Patterson, sentenced to 75 years in January 1936.

Plea in Powell Case

In making the announcement at the committee's office, 112 E. 19th St., Morris Shapiro, secretary of the committee, stated that the committee "would also use every legal recourse to also obtain the release" of Ozie Powell, the fifth imprisoned Scottsboro youth.

Powell pleaded "guilty" to a charge of "attacking" a deputy sheriff and received a sentence of 20 years at the Morgan County Circuit court two weeks ago. Every effort will be made to have Powell's sentence reduced as low as possible, Shapiro explained.

Notice of appeal had already been filed in the case of Clarence Norris by Samuel Leibowitz, chief Scottsboro defense attorney. The notice had the effect of a stay of execution for Norris, who over the long six-year period of the world famous cases has been sentenced to die three times.

Supreme Court

In the case of Patterson, Fraenkel moved for a writ of certiorari taking the case for its third journey to the United States Supreme Court. The writ is discretionary with the Supreme Court. The Alabama Supreme Court has already upheld Patterson's 75-year sentence.

Fraenkel, who has been associated with two previous successful Scottsboro appeals to the United States Supreme Court, was retained a third time after a joint conference between defense counsel Leibowitz, Shapiro, and Joseph Brodsky, head of the legal staff of the International Labor Defense.

In a statement issued immediately after the release of Olen Montgomery, Roy Wright, Willie Roberson and Eugene Williams, the four Scottsboro boys, the Scottsboro Committee said:

"Every legal recourse will be exhausted in pressing the appeals from the conviction of the imprisoned youths, looking to their acquittal and release."

In August 1937 Olen Montgomery, Eugene Williams, Roy Wright, and Willie Roberson appeared in a show in Harlem. Agitation for the freedom of the five in prison continued.

"Jailed Scottsboro Boys are Menaced by Prison Sickness"

Daily Worker

September 9, 1937

Ben Davis

A new menace—serious illness—brought on by almost seven years of harried and continuous confinement in the Alabama jails now threatens the lives of four of the five imprisoned Scottsboro boys, it was revealed yesterday.

Mrs. Ada Wright, who has just returned from a trip to Kilby prison in Montgomery, Ala., said yesterday that two of the boys were now confined in the prison hospital. Mrs. Wright's hurried trip was due to a request from her son Andy, who was recently operated on for acute hemorrhoids.

"Andy is going to have to be operated on again in a few days I'm afraid," she said.

Others Are Ill

Charlie Weems, sentenced to 75 years, has tuberculosis, while Haywood Patterson, also sentenced to 75 years, is suffering from a dangerous infection in his leg, Mrs. Wright stated. Patterson underwent an emergency operation about ten days ago.

"Ozie Powell," Mrs. Wright explained, "is hardly more than skin and bones. The boys say he is dying on his feet." Powell who is partially paralyzed in one side as a result of being shot in the head by a deputy sheriff in 1936, was sentenced to 20 years after a plea of guilty to an "attack" on the sheriff.

Simultaneously, Mrs. Wright urged all "friends of my son and the other Scottsboro boys to give all support to the Scottsboro Defense Committee in its efforts to free the remaining five boys. We must all work fast and hard—and together, for their long stay in prison is slowly sapping their lives."

Fears Loss of Arm

Mrs. Wright also the mother of Roy, one of the four freed Negro youths, visited Andy last Sunday. With her were her two daughters Beatrice Maddox and Lucille, who also reside in Chattanooga, Tenn.

"Andy said that he was to lose the use of his right arm from work about the prison which requires him to stand on his feet from six in the morning until six at night. He told me 'Mother, I'm sick and I can't stand this very long. Tell my friends to hurry and do all they can to get us out of here.'"

Andy, she stated, informed her of the condition of all the boys. "They don't allow any one to see the boys unless they are relatives. I tried to see Haywood Patterson, who stayed right around the block from me in Chattanooga, but they wouldn't let me because I wasn't any kin to him," Mrs. Wright continued.

Mrs. Janie Patterson, Haywood's mother, is unable to visit her son since suffering a stroke of paralysis at her home in Cincinnati, Ohio.

Clarence Norris, the fifth imprisoned youth, is confined in the Jefferson County jail. Norris is under a sentence of death.

Appeals Filed

Osmond K. Fraenkel, eminent constitutional attorney who handled two previous Scottsboro appeals, has already filed appeals in the cases of the imprisoned boys. Fraenkel was retained by the Scottsboro Defense Committee, 112 E. 19th St.

An application for a writ of certiorari in the case of Haywood Patterson, who was sentenced in January 1936, has been made to the United States Supreme Court by Fraenkel.

Meanwhile the Scottsboro Defense Committee, composed of eight national labor and progressive organizations, is in the midst of a campaign to secure defense funds and ten million signatures to a petition to Gov. Bibb Graves of Alabama urging immediate release of all five of the boys.

Angelo Herndon understood the plight of the Scottsboro youths better than anyone else because he, too, in the thirties had been unjustly accused, arrested, tried, and imprisoned by the white South. His 1937 pamphlet summarized the case up to that point and reflected the thoughts and emotions felt by many supporters of the defendants.

New York: Workers Library, 1937

"The Scottsboro Boys"

Pamphlet

August 1937

Angelo Herndon

Four Freed!

Five to Go!

Eugene Williams, Roy Wright, Willie Roberson and Olen Montgomery are free! Let this victory and great cause for jubilation hasten on the struggle for the freedom of the other five boys.

Six years of unyielding struggle of the Negro people, of their supporters, and of friends of democracy and justice the world over—in the U. S. A., London, Moscow, Berlin, Cuba, Mexico and Spain—have wrenched from the hands of Alabama's feudal despots four more intended victims of the rope and faggot.

Congratulations, International Labor Defense, the Communist Party, and the Young Communist League. Congratulations to the organizations of the united Scottsboro Defense Committee, the National Association for the Advancement of Colored People, the League for Industrial Democracy, the Church League for Industrial Democracy (Episcopal), the I.L.D., the Methodist Federation for Social Service and the American Civil Liberties Union. You have scored a smash-hit victory for Negro rights and the preservation of civil liberties

We of the Young Communist League are proud that we have played a leading role in this noble cause for justice and democracy. In expressing our greetings to the Scottsboro boys and their defenders, we pledge our continued efforts in mobilizing every possible force in the fight for the freedom of the other five. We shall be ever vigilant in bringing to the consciousness of all youth the shameful crime of Scottsboro. We will leave no stone unturned in the fight for the liberation of the Negro people from the rule of Southern landlord oppression.

Alabama's attempt to perpetuate the slave system by framing nine Negroes met with universal opposition from those who have been outraged by this crude type of injustice. The liberty-loving people of the world chorused in repeated determination: *The Scottsboro boys shall not die!* The hundreds and thousands of mass meetings, demonstrations and other dramatic actions struck a ringing blow at Alabama's system of human bondage.

The compelling force generated through the organized might of millions wrung from their bloodstained hands this glorious, but partial, victory.

On July 25, 1937, after six long years of endless and tireless work for the freedom of the Scottsboro boys, the news which flashed around the world that four of the boys had been freed came as a thunderbolt of joy and happiness to the hearts of millions. In Harlem, New York, many Negro mothers, who had untiringly followed the Scottsboro case from its beginning, wept for sheer joy. Kerchiefs in hand, they dabbed away almost incessantly at the tears that flowed freely until their warm hearts tired from the excitement. In their happiness, they expressed their kindred feeling of brotherhood with all the members of their race who are degraded and crushed by the iron heel of Southern barbarism. They wanted to share with these mothers the joy which now came after six years of grief and sorrow.

One Negro mother, in a sonorous voice, intoned: "Great God, Scottsboro boys are free! I knew the lynchers would never touch a hair in their heads. O, ye Scottsboro, shame of the lynchers' rule: we will never forget you—you who torture and burn black men! But we've cheated you—four lives you'll never get. O, Scottsboro, now we're wise—five more lives will never satisfy your ravenous thirst for black man's blood!"

Like this Negro mother, white trade unionists, liberals, clergymen, writers and all progressive people who believe that "all men are created equal" have understood that the fight to save the lives of the nine boys is a fight of progressive humanity against the barbarities of an age-worn slave system. The corrupt politicians and other shady characters have fought so stubbornly to send the boys to their death because they, too, have recognized that Scottsboro is a challenge to their vile system of political and economic servitude.

For six years, through falsehoods, intrigue, bribery and intimidation, the State of Alabama has insisted upon the supreme penalty of death for the boys. At the second trial of Haywood

Patterson, the late attorney general, Knight, after working himself up in a lather, in a thundering voice of hatred and contempt for the Negro people demanded of the jury:

"Send that black thing [Haywood Patterson—A.H.] to his death. Alabama justice cannot be bought with Jew money from New York."

Releasing Four to Murder Five

Of all the inconsistencies, one might be prompted to ask: why have the authorities of Alabama for six years held all nine of the boys guilty of the crime of rape and now, as if by some stroke of magic, they suddenly decided that five of them are innocent? The answer is that they have known from the very beginning that all of the boys are innocent.

In the case of Ozie Powell, Alabama has laid itself wide open for castigation. Ozie Powell was exonerated from all charges of rape and sentenced to twenty years for scratching Sheriff Sandlin's throat. The truth of the matter is that Ozie Powell, in almost insane desperation after more than five years of prison confinement, was provoked to defend himself from the taunts, jibes and physical maulings received from the hands of Sheriff Sandlin. Half of his brain was shot away—his whole body is practically paralyzed from the bullet that almost proved fatal to him. For this, Powell has been sentenced to twenty years. But, like a thief when caught in the act of committing some terrible crime, the authorities of Alabama have tried to wriggle out of a situation in which they have received scathing admonitions from the working class and prominent liberals. Yes, the whole world knows that the Scottsboro boys are not guilty. Nobody will be fooled by the insidious move of releasing four in order to murder the other five.

Victoria Price lied defiantly for six years. She swore by the Bible and everything else, as only a disreputable character like her would do, that all nine of the boys raped her in succession. According to her story at the first and other trials that followed, she was thrown on top of [a] sharp jagged rock, in the open gondola car in which they were riding, and the nine Negroes ravished her one after the other. Clearly the State of Alabama now admits that she was giving false testimony.

Dr. D.R. Bridges, who examined her, testified that there was no evidence of scratches or cuts on her back, no[r] of such injuries as would be expected after such an experience. It seems rather interesting in view of the fact that she claimed to have fought back vigorously in trying to keep the Negroes off, that there were no bruises or scratches on her back—a remarkable back she has! The examination of Victoria Price by Dr. Bridges on the day of the alleged rape indicated that she had not had intercourse for at least twenty-four hours.

Dr. Bridges also testified that she was calm and showed no signs of excitement such as would be inevitable after mass rape.

Ruby Bates Declares Boys Innocent

Ruby Bates, who repudiated her previous testimony, blasted the whole frameup when she testified that neither she nor Victoria Price had been touched by the nine Negroes. Since then Ruby Bates has been working for the freedom of the Scottsboro boys.

Her conscience would not allow her to be a tool of the white ruling class in sending nine innocent boys to death. The Scottsboro case had such a strong influence upon her that she has now dedicated her life to the fight for the freedom of the Scottsboro boys. Her deep-going experience with the attempt of the white slave masters to use her as a pawn in their dastardly game of oppression and exploitation caused her to recognize in this fight that only through the united efforts of the Negro and white workers can there be any real solution of their mutual problems. Such courage and heroism should serve as a symbol of greater solidarity in the struggle of Negro and white oppressed peoples.

But the State of Alabama concurred in Victoria Price's perjured testimony and held her up as a glowing example of true white womanhood. Upon the words of a habitual prostitute, whose purity of womanhood and character had long passed into obscurity, the lynchers sought to snuff out the lives of nine black boys.

The trial was a farce, as all the others have proved to be. Guilty or innocent, Alabama wanted nothing short of the death penalty. On April 8, 1931, an all-white jury found the boys guilty, and Judge Hawkins set the date of execution on July 10.

A United World-Wide Struggle

It was at this time that the I.L.D. stepped in and demanded a halt to this attempted wholesale massacre. It dispatched the following wire to Judge Hawkins and the Governor of Alabama:

> We demand stay of execution and opportunity to investigate and prepare for new trial or appeal. We demand right for our attorney to interview defendants and obtain approval of defense counsel. And above all, we demand absolutely safety for the defendants against 'lynching'.

Joseph Brodsky, chief counsel for the I.L.D., went down to Alabama and made application for the arrest of judgment against the boys. Upon his arrival, he was met by a howling mob of lynchers. In his efforts to have the convictions set aside, Hawkins immediately overruled Brodsky's request. Brodsky took exception to the judge's ruling, whereupon the judge overruled his exception. Brodsky then countered with an exception to Hawkins' decision overruling his previous request to except.

The judge became so angry that he made a grand exit through the rear door of the courtroom. In all the confusion, Brodsky turned round, and was suddenly seized by a husky man who said:

"Come on, yah Jew bitch! We'll show you how to defend nigger rapers."

When the execution date, July 10, was set aside, the I.L.D. mobilized all of its forces for a fight to the finish. J. Louis

Engdahl, late chairman of the I.L.D., with Mother Ada Wright, toured twenty-six European countries on behalf of the Scottsboro boys.

In Germany, Scotland, Czechoslovakia, Switzerland, Belgium and the Soviet Union, the message of Scottsboro was spread far and wide. In his sincere devotion and untiring work for the Scottsboro boys, Engdahl lost his health and died a few months later in Moscow from pneumonia.

The Communist Party and the Young Communist League were the great stimulating forces which brought Scottsboro before the broad masses of organized labor. In cooperation with the I.L.D., the question of Negro[es]serving on juries was raised for the first time. Because this question struck at the root of Negro oppression, and because of the mass fight carried on around it, the United States Supreme Court was forced to reverse the convictions of the Scottsboro boys for the second time. Like the infamous Dred Scott decision, in which the Negro-hating Judge Taney ruled that a Negro "had no rights a white man is bound to respect," Scottsboro became the beacon light and symbol of the struggle of the Negro for complete freedom.

All over the country, the Communist Party and the Young Communist League agitated and fought for the unity of all workers and progressive liberals in defense of the Scottsboro boys. Communists were jailed, terrorized and beaten for daring to protest against this gross travesty upon justice. In Chemnitz, Germany, two white Communists were killed in a demonstration for the Scottsboro boys.

Just as the pioneers of 1776 blazed the trails in search of democracy, freedom and a decent world for human beings to live in, so the Communists were the spearheads who first threw support around the Scottsboro case. Communists recognized that in order to wage an effective fight it was necessary to expose and publish abroad the denial of elementary human justice, the inhuman exploitation which has been invariably imposed upon the Negro by the bourbon ruling class of the South. We Communists are proud of the work that we initiated in the fight for the

Scottsboro boys. We will continue to pursue that course which must result in the freedom of the five remaining Scottsboro boys. In this connection, we want to point out that Samuel Leibowitz, Osmond K. Fraenkel, Walter Pollak and other lawyers have put up a brilliant and wonderful legal fight for the Scottsboro boys. But none of these alone could have freed the four boys nor can they free the other five as a lone fighter. Without the backing of millions behind the legal fight, the Scottsboro boys would already have moldered away in the graves.

The understanding of the real significance of the Scottsboro case, and the work which the Communists have carried on, has to an immeasurably large degree contributed to the freeing of four of the boys. The fight of the Communists in the trade unions for Negro rights and the decisive turn of thousands of Negroes to the unions of the Committee for Industrial Organization helped to crystallize the broad expression of varied sentiment which made possible this victory.

The Five Others Must Go Free

When the jail doors swung open, and Eugene Williams, Roy Wright, Willie Roberson, and Olen Montgomery walked out into the free, wide-open spaces, Alabama suffered a terrible defeat. By releasing the boys after six years of struggling desperately to get their blood, the authorities of Alabama admitted to the whole world that all nine of the boys are completely innocent of the charges for which they have given the best part of their youthful lives. Alabama has admitted its own guilt of wrongfully, willfully and intentionally persecuting and torturing these boys for six years in the shadow of the electric chair.

The Communist Party and the Young Communist League demand full compensation for every day of these boys' wasted and tortured lives. The authorities of Alabama are guilty of pre-meditating murder. They must be made to pay.

Communists pledge their continued support to the fight for the vindication of the other boys. One important victory has been won. This should stimulate even more and greater activity on the part of all who have thus far helped to make possible this partial victory. Those desiring to maintain liberty and democracy should redouble their efforts on behalf of the five Scottsboro boys who must be freed.

Protest resolutions and telegrams must flood the offices of Alabama authorities demanding the freedom of the Scottsboro boys. Funds with which to continue the fight are also needed. Contributions can be made to the Scottsboro Committee, 112 East 19th Street, New York City.

To the youth of our generation Scottsboro is a tragic lesson of what a future under reaction would hold in store. It spells death especially to the younger Negro generation. But through the victory of Scottsboro, a future which is bright with hope, confidence and the attributes of man's ability to abolish exploitation of man by man, can be realized.

When the history of the Scottsboro persecution and frameup is written it will go down in the shame and infamy which it has earned for itself. On the other hand, the lessons of Scottsboro will be a medium through which will be cemented indestructible bonds of unity between Negro and white workers.

But, to hasten Scottsboro on into the chambers of horror, it must be placed there without the satisfaction of having devoured five of its victims—with little or no opposition. The floodgates of our indignation must be let loose in torrents of protest that will make Alabama retreat in its aim to commit mass murder.

Therefore, the Young Communists of America urge the progressive youth of our country to give their unstinted support to the fight to save five of our brothers who share and suffer with us all the horrors of a dying world. Young Catholics, Gentiles, Jews, and Negro and white—Scottsboro is calling you! Five black boys—who have grown into manhood behind prison bars—need you! Will you lend them a hand? You cannot fail them—if you do this, then you are jeopardizing your own rights for a peaceful and happy existence in this world of ours.

To the Negro people, Communists pledge their undying loyalty and devotion to the cause for Negro emancipation—which is the struggle of all people who wish to be free. We recognize that the fight of any people for freedom and independence is not an easy one. The trials and tribulations which must be endured are tremendous. It took years of agitation and hard and painstaking work to crush the black monster of chattel slavery. There is no room for vacillation. Every hard-won victory must be followed up with even more determination; to the end that our goal shall soon be realized. Those who flinch and stand in the way of progress must be brushed aside.

In all worthy causes there are to be found Judases who would sell their brothers' flesh for thirty pieces of silver. Plagued with the irresistible itch to curry favor of their masters, nothing is too base for them to do. The work of such people is always utilized by the enemy to prevent any attempt at unity among those whom it exploits. The following words of Dr. G. Lake Imes, Secretary of Tuskegee Institute, are being used by Alabama authorities to break the unity of the Negro people in their fight for the Scottsboro boys:

"We can look to the white man in the South for justice—it makes me feel proud to be a citizen of Alabama. I was one of the volunteer committee that went to Kilby Prison and pleaded in vain with these Scottsboro boys to put their cases in the hands of Alabama attorneys."

When servile creatures of that type are at the head of institutions of learning is it any wonder that the road of Negro liberation is beset with damnable obstacles[?]

Perhaps Mr. Imes does not know that the slave masters of the South realize full well that their institutions of slavery are built upon volcanoes, which may burst forth at any moment, and give freedom to their victims. That is why they are so persistent in their efforts to burn the Scottsboro boys. It is for the same reason that they point to such Negroes who always want to "trust their interests to the good will" of their white rulers. They seek through such means to demobilize all the energies of the Negro people. But this only points to the heinous crimes which the slave lords wish to cover up.

It is another indictment of their vile system of economic robbery.

There shall be no compromise in the fight to free the five remaining boys. The boys are innocent and they must go free.

Epilogue

Epilogue

Negotiations for the release of the five Scottsboro defendants still in prison continued throughout 1938. The united front forces sustained their agitation for the freedom of the Scottsboro victims into the 1940s. On February 20, 1942, the Alabama Pardons Board denied pardon to Clarence Norris and Charles Weems. In light of the military conflict in Europe during World War II, the nation became preoccupied with the war effort and interest in the Scottsboro case waned. The Scottsboro Defense Committee grew inactive. Its chairperson, Allan Knight Chalmers, maintained minimal contact with the International Labor Defense. The ILD, for its part, sent a monthly sum to each Scottsboro defendant still imprisoned.

On January 8, 1944, Andrew Wright (30 years old) and Clarence Norris (32 years old), were paroled. Charles Weems (33) was paroled later. Norris, out nine months, was re-imprisoned as a parole violator. Let out again in 1947, Norris headed North. Wright was returned twice to prison as a parole violator. Authorities paroled Ozie Powell on June 16, 1946. He moved to Georgia.

In April 1947, the International Labor Defense merged with the National Federation for Constitutional Liberties and the Veterans Against Discrimination. Together they formed the Civil Rights Congress (CRC). The CRC continued contact with Haywood Patterson and Andrew Wright. On July 17, 1948, Haywood Patterson escaped from Kilby Prison. In June 1950 Andy Wright was paroled to New York. The FBI arrested Haywood Patterson in Detroit. In August 1952 Haywood Patterson died. In 1959 Roy Wright tragically committed suicide. In 1976 Alabama Governor George Wallace pardoned Clarence Norris. In 1989, the last of the Scottsboro boys, Clarence Norris, died.

Profiles of Black Communists

Amis, B. D. (1896–1993) is virtually unknown today and often overlooked by historians. As an African American Communist, he was a major figure in the black freedom struggle during the two decades between the world wars. At that time, the American Communist Party played a significant role in fighting for the rights of African Americans. This was especially true during the Party's heyday in the late 1920s and the 1930s. In those years, Amis was, to be sure, part of the small circle of black radicals leading the struggle for workers' rights and racial justice. In 1930, Amis became the general secretary of the newly formed League of Struggle for Negro Rights and editor of its organ, *The Liberator.* The League publicized the racial issues of the day such as lynching, rallies, conferences, and picketing. Aptly described as "urbane in demeanor and a dynamic speaker," he was indeed one of the most important black activists of his time. His daughter, Debbie A. Bell, is the Chairperson of the Eastern Pennsylvania/Delaware District of the Communist Party, USA. B. D. Amis died in Virginia in 1993.

Briggs, Cyril (1888–1966) was an African American Communist leader and a writer. Born in the Caribbean he moved as a young man to Harlem and soon became a black journalist. He founded the African Blood Brotherhood in 1917 to fight against lynching, segregation, disenfranchisement, and the American racial caste system. Briggs joined the American Communist Party in 1921 and soon became an antagonist of black nationalist Marcus Garvey. Briggs died in 1966 in Los Angeles.

Davis, Benjamin J., Jr. (1903–1964) rose from his birth in Georgia to become an African American civil rights lawyer, a New York City councilman, an author and editor, a Marxist theoretician, and a leader in the American Communist Party. After graduating from Amherst College (1929) and the Harvard Law School (1932), young Davis joined the Communist Party in 1933 during his legal defense of Angelo Herndon (a young African American Communist organizer who faced the death penalty in Georgia). After moving to New York City in the mid-1930s, he served as the editor/publisher of the *Daily Worker* and its successor, the weekly *The Worker,* and as a member of the editorial board of *Political Affairs,* the theoretical journal of the Communist Party. He is also the author of an extensive autobiography and of several pamphlets on Communism and blacks. Elected to the New York City Council as a Harlem representative in 1943, Davis was one of two Communist Party candidates to have ever been elected to office in the United States. In 1949, Davis was one of eleven Communist leaders convicted of conspiring to overthrow the United States government. At the time of his death in 1964 Davis was under indictment (McCarran Act) for his refusal to register as an agent of the Soviet Union.

Ford, James W. (1893–1957) was a Harlem Communist who became a major Party organizer in New York City. As the first African American to appear on a presidential ticket in the United States during the twentieth century, he served as the American Communist Party's vice-presidential candidate in the 1932, 1936, and 1940 elections.

Gordon, Eugene (1891–1974), an African American journalist and writer born in Florida in 1891 who studied English and journalism at Howard and Boston Universities, was one of the co-founders of the Boston John Reed Club. He joined the American Communist Party in 1931 and during the 1930s worked in the Soviet Union as a reporter for the "Moscow Daily News." He also worked in the 1930s and 1940s for the *Daily Worker* as a feature editor, reporter, and writer. He continued to write as a leftist until his death until 1974.

Haywood, Harry (1898–1978), born in Nebraska as a son of a former slave, was a member of the African Blood Brotherhood and the Young Workers League before he joined the American Communist Party in 1925. After traveling to the Soviet Union and studying Marxism at the Lenin School in Moscow, Haywood became one of the party's chief black theorists. He is credited with influencing the Communist International in 1928 to define black Americans as an "oppressed nation." He was in on the formation of the League of Struggle for Negro Rights, and served in the

Abraham Lincoln Battalion as well as the U.S. Merchant Marine in WWII. He died in 1978.

Herndon, Angelo (1913–1997), was born into poverty into a small Ohio town and during the Great Depression the fight against unemployment led him to join the American Communist Party. As a "true believer," Herndon organized for the Party in the 1930s. In Atlanta, Georgia as he led a large, militant hunger march he came to the attention of legal authorities. He was charged, arrested, and tried with the crime of violating the anti-radical, insurrection law in the state of Georgia. The International Labor Defense came to his rescue, paid his bail, and defended him in court. After an all-white jury found him guilty, he was sentenced to 18–20 years in prison. His case was unsuccessfully appealed to Georgia's Supreme Court; however, in 1937 his conviction was overturned by the U.S. Supreme Court.

Padmore, George (1902–1959), born in Trinidad, was at various times in his life an author, a communist, and a pan-African theorist. His given name was Malcolm Ivan Meredith Nurse. During the 1920s in the United States he studied at Columbia, Fisk, Howard, and New York University. He joined the American Communist Party in 1927 and served as a journalist as well as head of the Negro Bureau of the Red International of Labor Unions and the International Trade Union Committee of Negro Workers. After disagreeing with Party leaders in the early 1930s, Padmore was expelled and then turned his attention to developing his Pan-African views through a series of books and other writings. He became a close associate of Ghana's Kwame Nkrumah in the 1950s and died in 1959.

Patterson, William L. (1890–1980) was a major African American leader in the Communist Party, USA, and led the International Labor Defense, an auxiliary of the Party that provided legal representation to Communists, labor activists, and African Americans in cases that involved political and racial mistreatment. Later active in the Civil Rights Congress, in 1951 he offered the noted petition to the United Nations, *We Charge Genocide: The Crime of Government Against the Negro People*. He continued to work for civil rights until his death in 1980.

Appendix

I. The 1928 Comintern Resolution on the Negro Question in the United States

1. The industrialization of the South, the concentration of a new Negro working class population in the big cities of the East and North and the entrance of the Negroes into the basic industries on a mass scale, create the possibility for the Negro workers, under the leadership of the Communist Party, to assume the hegemony of all Negro liberation movements, and to increase their importance and role in the revolutionary struggle of the American proletariat.

   The Negro working class has reached a stage of development which enables it, if properly organized and well led, to fulfill successfully its double historical mission:

   (a) To play a considerable role in the class struggle against American imperialism as an important part of the American working class; and

   (b) To lead the movement of the oppressed masses of the Negro population.

2. The bulk of the Negro population (86%) live in the southern states; of this number 74 per cent live in the rural districts and are dependent almost exclusively upon agriculture for a livelihood. Approximately one-half of these rural dwellers live in the so-called "Black Belt," in which area they constitute more than

50 per cent of the entire population. The great mass of the Negro agrarian population are subject to the most ruthless exploitation and persecution of a semi-slave character. In addition to the ordinary forms of capitalist exploitation, American imperialism utilizes every possible form of slave exploitation (peonage, share-cropping, landlord supervision of crops and marketing, etc.) for the purpose of extracting super-profits. On the basis of these slave remnants, there has grown up a super-structure of social and political inequality that expresses itself in Lynching, segregation, Jim Crowism, etc.

Necessary Conditions for National Revolutionary Movement

3. The various forms of oppression of the Negro masses, who are concentrated mainly in the so-called "Black Belt," provide the necessary conditions for a national revolutionary movement among the Negroes. The Negro agricultural laborers and the tenant farmers feel most the pressure of white persecution and exploitation. Thus, the agrarian problem lies at the root of the Negro national movement. The great majority of Negroes in the rural districts of the South are not "reserves of capitalist reaction," but potential allies of the revolutionary proletariat. Their objective position facilitates their transformation into a revolutionary force, which, under the leadership of the proletariat, will be able to participate in the joint struggle with all other workers against capitalist exploitation.

4. It is the duty of the Negro workers to organize through the mobilization of the broad masses of the Negro population the struggle of the agricultural laborers and tenant farmers against all forms of semi-feudal oppression. On the other hand, it is the duty of the Communist Party of the U.S.A. to mobilize and rally the broad masses of the white workers for active participation in this struggle. For that reason the Party must consider the beginning of systematic work in the South as one of its main tasks, having regard for the fact that the bringing together of the workers and toiling masses of all nationalities for a joint struggle against the landowners and the bourgeoisie is one of the most important aims of the Communist International, as laid down in the resolutions on the national and colonial question of the Second and Sixth Congresses of the Comintern.

For Complete Emancipation of Oppressed Negro Race

5. To accomplish this task, the Communist Party must come out as the champion of the right of the oppressed Negro race for full emancipation. While continuing and intensifying the struggle under the slogan of full social and political equality for the Negroes, which must remain the central slogan of our Party for work among the masses, the Party must come out openly and unreservedly for the right of the Negroes to national self-determination in the southern states, where the Negroes form a majority of the population. The struggle for equal rights and the propaganda for the slogan of self-determination must be linked up with the economic demands of the Negro masses, especially those directed against the slave remnants and all forms of national and racial oppression. Special stress must be laid upon organizing active resistance against Lynching, Jim Crowism, segregation and all other forms of oppression of the Negro population.

6. All work among the Negroes, as well as the struggle for the Negro cause among the whites, must be used, based upon the changes which have taken place in the relationship of classes among the Negro population. The existence of a Negro industrial proletariat of almost two million workers makes it imperative that the main emphasis should be placed on these new proletarian forces. The Negro workers must be organized under the leadership of the Communist Party, and thrown into joint struggle together with the white workers. The Party must learn to combine all demands of the Negroes with the economic and political struggle of the workers and the poor farmers.

American Negro Question Part of World Problem

7. The Negro question in the United States must be treated in its relation to the Negro questions and struggles in other parts of the world. The Negro race everywhere is an oppressed race. Whether it is a minority (U.S.A., etc.), majority (South Africa) or inhabits a so-called independent state (Liberia, etc.), the Negroes are oppressed by imperialism. Thus, a common tie of interest is established for the revolutionary struggle of race and national liberation from imperialist domination of the Negroes in various parts of the world. A strong Negro revolutionary movement in the U.S.A. will be able to influence and direct the

revolutionary movement in all those parts of the world where the Negroes are oppressed by imperialism.

8. The proletarianization of the Negro masses makes the trade unions the principal form of mass organization. It is the primary task of the Party to play an active part and lead in the work of organizing the Negro workers and agricultural laborers in trade unions. Owing to the refusal of the majority of the white unions in the U.S.A., led by the reactionary leaders, to admit Negroes to membership, steps must be immediately taken to set up special unions for those Negro workers who are not allowed to join the white unions. At the same time, however, the struggles for the inclusion of Negro workers in the existing unions must be intensified and concentrated upon, special attention must be given to those unions in which the statutes and rules set up special limitations against the admission of Negro workers. Primary duty of Communist Party in this connection is to wage a merciless struggle against the A.F. of L. bureaucracy, which prevents the Negro workers from joining the white workers' unions. The organization of special trade unions for the Negro masses must be carried out as part and parcel of the struggle against the restrictions imposed upon the Negro workers and for their admission to the white workers' unions. The creation of separate Negro unions should in no way weaken the struggle in the old unions for the admission of Negroes on equal terms. Every effort must be made to see that all the new unions organized by the Left wing and by the Communist Party should embrace the workers of all nationalities and of all races. The principle of one union for all workers in each industry, white and black, should cease to be a mere slogan of propaganda, and must become a slogan of action.

Party Trade Union Work Among Negroes

9. While organizing the Negroes into unions and conducting an aggressive struggle against the anti-Negro trade union policy of the A.F. of L., the Party must pay more attention than it has hitherto done to the work in the Negro workers' organizations, such as the Brotherhood of Sleeping Car Porters, Chicago Asphalt Workers' Union, and so on. The existence of two million Negro workers and the further industrialization of the Negroes demand a radical change in the work of the Party among the Negroes. The creation of working class organizations and the extension of our influence in the existing working class Negro

organizations, are of much greater importance than the work in bourgeois and petty-bourgeois organizations, such as the National Association for the Advancement of Colored People, the Pan-African Congress, etc.

10. The American Negro Labor Congress continues to exist only nominally. Every effort should be made to strengthen this organization as a medium through which we can extend the work of the Party among the Negro masses and mobilize the Negro workers under our leadership. After careful preparatory work, which must be started at once, another convention of the American Negro Labor Congress should be held. A concrete plan must also be presented to the Congress for an intensified struggle for the economic, social, political and national demands of the Negro masses. The program of the American Negro Labor Congress must deal specially with the agrarian demands of the Negro farmers and tenants in the South.

11. The importance of trade union work imposes special tasks upon the Trade Union Educational League. The T.U.E.L. has completely neglected the work among the Negro workers, notwithstanding the fact that these workers are objectively in a position to play a very great part in carrying through the program of organizing the unorganized. The closest contact must be established between the T.U.E.L. and the Negro masses. The T.U.E.L. must become the champion in the struggle for the rights of the Negroes in the old unions, and in the organizing of new unions for both Negroes and whites, as well as separate Negro unions.

White Chauvinism Evidenced in the American Party

The C.E.C. of the American Communist Party itself stated in its resolution of April 30, 1928, that "the Party as a whole has not sufficiently realized the significance of work among the Negroes." Such an attitude toward the Party work among the Negroes is, however, not satisfactory. The time is ripe to begin within the Party a courageous campaign of self-criticism concerning the work among the Negroes. Penetrating self-criticism is the necessary preliminary condition for directing the Negro work along new lines.

13. The Party must bear in mind that white chauvinism, which is the expression of the ideological influence of American imperialism among the workers, not only prevails among different strata of the white workers in the U.S.A., but is even reflected in

various forms in the Party itself. White chauvinism has manifested itself even in open antagonism of some comrades to the Negro comrades. In some instances where Communists were called upon to champion and to lead in the most vigorous manner the fight against white chauvinism, they instead yielded to it. In Gary, white members of the Workers Party protested against Negroes eating in the restaurant controlled by the Party. In Detroit, Party members, yielding to pressure, drove out Negro comrades from a social given in aid of the miners on strike. Whilst the Party has taken certain measures against these manifestations of white chauvinism, nevertheless those manifestations must be regarded as indications of race prejudice even in the ranks of the Party, which must be fought with the utmost energy.

14. An aggressive fight against all forms of white chauvinism must be accompanied by a widespread and thorough educational campaign in the spirit of internationalism within the Party, utilizing for this purpose to the fullest possible extent the Party schools, the Party press and the public platform, to stamp out all forms of antagonism, or even indifference among our white comrades toward the Negro work. This educational work should be conducted simultaneously with a campaign to draw the white workers and the poor farmers into the struggle for the support of the demands of the Negro workers.

Tasks of Party in Relation to Negro Work

15. The Communist Party of the U.S.A. in its treatment of the Negro question must all the time bear in mind this twofold task:

    (a) To fight for the full rights of the oppressed Negroes and for their right to self-determination and against all forms of chauvinism, especially among the workers of the oppressing nationality.

    (b) The propaganda and the day-to-day practice of international class solidarity must be considered as one of the basic tasks of the American Communist Party. The fight—by propaganda and by deeds—should be directed first and foremost against the chauvinism of the workers of the oppressing nationality as well as against bourgeois segregation tendencies of the oppressed nationality. The propaganda of international class solidarity is the necessary prerequisite for the unity of the working class in the struggle.

"The center of gravity in educating the workers of the oppressing countries in the principles of internationalism must inevitably consist in the propaganda and defense by these workers of the right of segregation by the oppressed countries. We have the right and duty to treat every socialist of an oppressing nation, who does not conduct such propaganda, as an imperialist and as a scoundrel." (Lenin, selected articles on the national question.)

16. The Party must seriously take up the task of training a cadre of Negro comrades as leaders, bring them into the Party schools in the U.S.A. and abroad, and make every effort to draw Negro proletarians into active and leading work in the Party, not confining the activities of the Negro comrades exclusively to the work among Negroes. Simultaneously, white workers must specially be trained for work among the Negroes.

17. Efforts must be made to transform the "Negro Champion" into a weekly mass organ of the Negro proletariat and tenant farmers. Every encouragement and inducement must be given to the Negro comrades to utilize the Party press generally.

Negro Work Part of General Work of Party

18. The Party must link up the struggle on behalf of the Negroes with the general campaigns of the Party. The Negro problem must be part and parcel of all and every campaign conducted by the Party. In the election campaigns, trade union work, the campaigns for the organization of the unorganized, anti-imperialist work, labor party campaign, International Labor Defense, etc., the Central Executive Committee must work out plans designed to draw the Negroes into active participation in all these campaigns, and at the same time to bring the white workers into the struggle on behalf of the Negroes' demands. It must be borne in mind that the Negro masses will not be won for the revolutionary struggles until such time as the most conscious section of the white workers show, by action, that they are fighting with the Negroes against all racial discrimination and persecution. Every member of the Party must bear in mind that "the age-long oppression of the colonial and weak nationalities by the imperialist powers, has given rise to a feeling of bitterness among the masses of the enslaved countries as well as a feeling of distrust toward the oppressing nations in general and toward the proletariat of those nations."

19. The Negro women in industry and on the farms constitute a powerful potential force in the struggle for Negro emancipation. By reason of being unorganized to an even greater extent than male Negro workers, they are the most exploited section. The A.F. of L. bureaucracy naturally exercises toward them a double hostility, by reason of both their color and sex. It therefore becomes an important task of the Party to bring the Negro women into the economic and political struggle.

20. Only by an active and strenuous fight on the part of the white workers against all forms of oppression directed against the Negroes, will the Party be able to draw into its ranks the most active and conscious Negro workers—men and women—and to increase its influence in those intermediary organizations which are necessary for the mobilization of the Negro masses in the struggle against segregation, lynching, Jim Crowism, etc.

21. In the present struggle in the mining industry, the Negro workers participate actively and in large numbers. The leading role the Party played in this struggle has helped greatly to increase its prestige. Nevertheless, the special efforts being made by the Party in the work among the Negro strikers cannot be considered as adequate. The Party did not send enough Negro organizers into the coalfields, and it did not sufficiently attempt, in the first stages of the fight, to develop the most able Negro strikers and to place them in leading positions. The Party must be especially criticized for its failure to put Negro workers on the Presidium of the Pittsburgh Miners' Conference, doing so only after such representation was demanded by the Negroes themselves.

22. In the work among the Negroes, special attention should be paid to the role played by the churches and preachers who are acting on behalf of American imperialism. The Party must conduct a continuous and carefully worked out campaign among the Negro masses, sharpened primarily against the preachers and the churchmen, who are the agents of the oppressors of the Negro race.

Party Work Among Negro Proletariat and Peasantry

23. The Party must apply united front tactics for specific demands to the existing Negro petty bourgeois organizations. The purpose of these united front tactics should be the mobilizing of the Negro masses under the leadership of the Party, and to expose the treacherous petty bourgeois leadership of those organizations.

24. The Negro Miners Relief Committee and the Harlem Tenants League are examples of joint organizations of action which may serve as a means of drawing the Negro masses into struggle. In every case the utmost effort must be made to combine the struggle of the Negro workers with the struggle of the white workers, and to draw the white workers' organizations into such joint campaigns.

25. In order to reach the bulk of the Negro masses, special attention should be paid to the work among the Negroes in the South. For that purpose, the Party should establish a district organization in the most suitable locality in the South. Whilst continuing trade union work among the Negro workers and the agricultural laborers, special organizations of tenant farmers must be set up. Special efforts must also be made to secure the support of the share croppers in the creation of such organizations. The Party must undertake the task of working out a definite program of immediate demands, directed against all slave remnants, which will serve as the rallying slogans for the formation of such peasant organizations.

Henceforth the Workers (Communist) Party must consider the struggle on behalf of the Negro masses, the task of organizing the Negro workers and peasants and the drawing of these oppressed masses into the proletarian revolutionary struggle, as one of its major tasks, remembering, in the words of the Second Congress resolution, that "the victory over capitalism cannot be fully achieved and carried to its ultimate goal unless the proletariat and the toiling masses of all nations of the world rally of their own accord in a concordant and close union."

II. The 1930 Comintern Resolution on the Negro Question in the United States

The C.P. of the United States has always acted openly and energetically against Negro oppression, and has thereby won increasing sympathy among the Negro population. In its own ranks, too, the Party has relentlessly fought the slightest evidences of white chauvinism, and has purged itself of the gross opportunism of the Lovestoneites. According to the assertions of these people, the "industrial revolution" will sweep away the remnants of slavery in the agricultural South, and will proletarianise the Negro peasantry, so that the Negro question, as a special national question, would thereby be presumably solved, or could be put off until the time of the socialist revolution in America. But the Party has not yet succeeded in overcoming in its own ranks all under-estimation of the struggle for the slogan of the right of self-determination, and still less succeeded in doing away with all *lack of clarity* on the Negro question. In the Party discussion the question was often wrongly put and much erroneous counter-posing of phrases of the question occurred, thus, for instance, should the slogan of social equality or the slogan of the right of self-determination of the Negroes be emphasized? Should only propaganda for the Negroes' right to self-determination be carried on, or should this slogan be considered as a slogan of action; should separatist tendencies among the Negroes be supported or opposed; is the Southern region, thickly populated by Negroes, to be looked upon as a colony, or as an "integral part of the national economy of the United States," where presumably a revolutionary situation cannot arise independent of the general revolutionary development in the United States?

In the interest of the utmost clarity of ideas on this question[,] the Negro question in the United States must be viewed from the standpoint of its peculiarity, namely as the question of an *oppressed nation*, which is in a peculiar and extraordinarily distressing situation of national oppression not only in view of the prominent *racial distinctions* (marked difference in the colour of skin, etc.), but above all because of considerable *social antagonism* (remnants of slavery). This introduces into the American Negro question an important, *peculiar* trait which is absent from the national question of other oppressed peoples. Furthermore, it is necessary to face clearly the inevitable distinction between the position of the Negro in the *South* and in the *North*, owing to the fact that at least three-fourths of the entire Negro population of the United States (12 million) live in compact masses in the South, most of them being peasants and agricultural labourers in a state of semi-serfdom, settled in the "Black Belt" and constituting the majority of the population, whereas the Negroes in the Northern States are for the most part industrial workers of the lowest categories who have recently come to the various industrial centres from the South (having often even fled from there).

The struggle of the Communists for the equal rights of the Negroes applies to all Negroes, in the North as well as in the South. The struggle for this slogan embraces all or almost all of the important special interests of the Negroes in the North, but not in the South, where the main Communist slogan must be: *The right of self-determination of the Negroes in the Black Belt.* These two slogans, however, are most closely connected. The Negroes in the North are very much interested in winning the right of self-determination for the Negro population of the Black Belt and can thereby hope for strong support for the establishment of true equality of the Negroes in the North. In the South the Negroes are suffering no less but still more than in the North from the glaring lack of all equality; for the most part the struggle for their most urgent partial demands in the Black Belt is nothing more than the struggle for their equal rights, and only the fulfillment of their main slogan, the right of self-determination in the Black Belt, can assure them of true equality.

The Struggle for the Equal Rights of the Negroes

2. [*There is no item 1.*] The basis for the demand of equality of the Negroes is provided by the special yoke to which the Negroes in the United States are subjected by the ruling classes. In comparison with the situation of the other various nationalities and faces oppressed by American imperialism, the yoke of the Negroes in the United States is of a peculiar nature and particularly oppressive. This is partly due to the historical past of the American Negroes as imported slaves, but is much more due to the still existing slavery of the American Negro which is immediately apparent, for example, in comparing their situation even with the situation of the Chinese and Japanese workers in the West of the United States, or with the lot of the Philippinos (Malay race) who are under colonial repression.

It is only a Yankee bourgeois lie to say that the yoke of Negro slavery has been lifted in the United States. Formally it has been abolished, but in practice the great majority of the Negro masses in the South are living in slavery in the literal sense of the word. Formally, they are "free" as "tenant farmers" or "contract labourers" on the big plantations of the white landowners, but actually, they are completely in the power of their exploiters; they are not permitted, or else it is made impossible for them to leave their exploiters; if they do leave the plantations, they are brought back and in many cases whipped; many of them are simply taken prisoner under various pretexts and, bound together with long chains, they have to do compulsory labour on the roads. All through the South, the Negroes are not only deprived of all rights, and subjected to the arbitrary will of the white exploiters, but they are also socially ostracized, that is, they are treated in general not as human beings, but as cattle. But this ostracism regarding Negroes is not limited to the South. Not only in the South but throughout the United States, the lynching of Negroes is permitted to go unpunished. Everywhere the American bourgeoisie surrounds the Negroes with an atmosphere of social ostracism.

The 100 per cent Yankee arrogance divides the American population into a series of castes, among which the Negroes constitute, so to speak, the caste of the "untouchables," who are in a still lower category than the lowest categories of human society, the immigrant labourers, the yellow immigrants and the Indians. In all big cities the Negroes have to live in special segregated ghettoes (and, of course, have to pay extremely high rent). In practice, marriage between Negroes and whites is prohibited, and in the South this is even forbidden by law. In various other ways, the Negroes are segregated, and if they overstep the bounds of the segregation they immediately run the risk of being ill-treated by the 100 per cent bandits. As wage-earners, the Negroes are forced to perform the lowest and most difficult work; they generally receive lower wages than the white workers and don't always get the same wages as white workers doing similar work, and their treatment is the very worst. Many A.F. of L. trade unions do not admit Negro workers in their ranks, and a number have organised special trade unions for Negroes so that they will not have to let them into their "good white society."

This whole system of "segregation" and "Jim Crowism" is a special form of national and social oppression under which the American Negroes have much to suffer. The origin of all this is not difficult to find: this Yankee arrogance towards the Negroes stinks of the disgusting atmosphere of the old slave market. This is downright robbery and slave-whipping barbarism at the peak of capitalist "culture."

3. The demand for equal rights in our sense of the word means not only demanding the same rights for the Negroes as the whites have in the United States at the present time but also demanding that the Negroes should be granted all rights and other advantages which we demand for the corresponding oppressed classes of whites (workers and other toilers). Thus in our sense of the word, the demand for equal rights means a continuous work of abolishment of all forms of economic and political oppression of the Negroes, as well as their social exclusion, the insults perpetrated against them and their segregation. This is to be obtained by constant struggle by the white and black workers for effective legal protection for the Negroes in all fields, as well as actual enforcement of their equality and combating of every expression of Negrophobia. One of the first Communist slogans is: Death for Negro lynching!

    The struggle for the equal rights of the Negroes does not in any way exclude recognition and support for the Negroes' rights to their own special schools, government organs, etc., wherever the

Negro masses put forward such national demands of their own accord. This will, however, in all probability occur to any great extent only in the Black Belt. In other parts of the country, the Negroes suffer above all from being shut out from the general social institutions and not from being prohibited to set up their own national institutions. With the development of the Negro intellectuals (principally in the "free" professions) and of a thin layer of small capitalist business people, there have appeared lately, not only definite efforts for developing a purely national Negro culture but also outspoken bourgeois tendencies towards Negro nationalism. The broad masses of the Negro population in the big industrial centres of the North are, however, making no efforts whatsoever to maintain and cultivate a national aloofness, they are, on the contrary, working for assimilation. This effort of the Negro masses can do much in the future to facilitate the progressive process of amalgamating the whites and Negroes into one nation, and it is under no circumstances the task of the Communists to give support to bourgeois nationalism in its fight with the progressive assimilation tendencies of the Negro working masses.

4. The slogan of equal rights of the Negroes *without a relentless struggle in practice against all manifestations of Negrophobia on the part of the American bourgeoisie* can be nothing but a deceptive liberal gesture of a sly slave-owner or his agent. This slogan is in fact repeated by "socialist" and many other bourgeois politicians and philanthropists who want to get publicity for themselves by appealing to the "sense of justice" of the American bourgeoisie in the individual treatment of the Negroes, and thereby sidetrack attention from the one effective struggle against the shameful system of "white superiority": from the *class struggle against the American bourgeoisie*. The struggle for equal rights for the Negroes is in fact, one of the most important parts of the proletarian class struggle of the United States.

The struggle for the equal rights for the Negroes must certainly take the form of common struggle by the white and black workers.

The increasing unity of the various working-class elements provokes constant attempts on the part of the American bourgeoisie to play one group against another, particularly the white workers against the black and the black workers against the immigrant workers and vice versa, and thus to promote divisions within the working-class, which contributes to the bolstering up of American capitalist rule. The Party must carry on a ruthless struggle against all these attempts of the bourgeoisie and do everything to strengthen the bonds of class solidarity of the working-class upon a lasting basis.

In the struggle for equal rights for the Negroes, however, it is the duty of the *white* workers to march at *the head* on this struggle. They must everywhere make a breach in the walls of segregation and "Jim Crowism" which have been set up by bourgeois slave-market morality. They must most ruthlessly unmask and condemn the hypocritical reformists and bourgeois "friends of Negroes" who, in reality, are only interested in strengthening the power of the enemies of the Negroes. They, the white workers, must boldly jump at the throat of the 100 per cent bandits who strike a Negro in the face. This struggle will be the test of the real international solidarity of the American white workers.

It is the special duty of the revolutionary Negro workers to carry on tireless activity among the Negro working masses to free them of their distrust of the white proletariat and draw them into the common front of the revolutionary class struggle against the bourgeoisie. They must emphasize with all force that the first rule of proletarian morality is that no worker who wants to be an equal member of his class must ever serve as a strike-breaker or a supporter of bourgeois politics. They must ruthlessly unmask all Negro politicians corrupted or directly bribed by American bourgeois ideology, who systematically interfere with the real proletarian struggle for the equal rights for the Negroes.

Furthermore, the Communist Party must resist all tendencies within its own ranks to ignore the Negro question as a national question in the United States, not only in the South, but also in the North. It is advisable for the Communist Party in the North to abstain from the establishment of any special Negro organisations, and in place of this to bring the black and white workers together in common organisations of struggle and joint action. Effective steps must be taken for the organisation of Negro workers in the T.U.U.L. and revolutionary trade unions. Under-estimation of this work takes. various forms: lack of energy in recruiting Negro workers, in keeping them in our ranks and in drawing them into the full life of the trade unions, in selecting, educating and promoting Negro forces to leading functions in the organisation. The Party must make itself entirely responsible for the carrying through of this very important work. It is most urgently necessary to publish a popular mass paper dealing with the Negro question, edited by white and black comrades, and to have all active followers of this paper grouped organisationally.

The Struggle for the Right of Self-determination of the Negroes in the Black Belt

5. It is not correct to consider the Negro zone of the South as a colony of the United States. Such a characterisation of the Black Belt could be based in some respects only upon artificially construed analogies, and would create superfluous difficulties for the clarification of ideas. In rejecting this estimation, however, it should not be overlooked that it would be none the less false to try to make a fundamental distinction between the character of national oppression to which the colonial peoples are subjected and the yoke of other oppressed nations. Fundamentally, national oppression in both cases is of the same character, and is in the Black Belt in many respects worse than in a number of actual colonies. On the one hand the Black Belt is not in itself, either economically or politically, such a united whole as to warrant its being called a special colony of the United States, but on the other hand this zone is not, either economically or politically, such an integral part of the whole United States as any other part of the country. Industrialisation in the Black Belt is not, as is generally the case in colonies properly speaking, in contradiction with the ruling interests of the imperialist bourgeoisie, which has in its hands the monopoly of the entire industry, but in so far as industry is developed here, it will in no way bring a solution to the question of living conditions of the oppressed Negro majority, or to the agrarian question, which lies at the basis of the national question. On the contrary, this question is still further aggravated as a result of the increase of the contradictions arising from the pre-capitalist forms of exploitation of the Negro peasantry and of a considerable portion of the Negro proletariat (miners, forestry workers, etc.) in the Black Belt, and at the same time owing to the industrial development here, the growth of the most important driving force of the national revolution, the black working-class, is especially strengthened. Thus, the prospect for the future is not an inevitable dying away of the national revolutionary Negro movement in the South, as Lovestone prophesied, but on the contrary, a great advance of this movement and the rapid approach of a revolutionary crisis in the Black Belt.

6. Owing to the peculiar situation in the Black Belt (the fact that the majority of the resident Negro population are farmers and agricultural labourers and that the capitalist economic system as well as political class rule there is not only of a special kind, but to a great extent still has pre-capitalist and semi-colonial features), the right of self-determination of the Negroes as the main slogan of the Communist Party in the Black Belt is appropriate. This, however, does not in any way mean that the struggle for equal rights of the Negroes in the Black Belt is less necessary or less well founded than it is in the North. On the contrary, here, owing to the whole situation, this struggle is even better founded, but the form of this slogan does not sufficiently correspond with the concrete requirements of the liberation struggle of the Negro population. Anyway, it is clear that in most cases it is a question of the daily conflicts of interest between the Negroes and the white rulers in the Black Belt on the subject of infringement of the most elementary equality rights of the Negroes by the whites. Daily events of the kind are: all Negro persecutions, all arbitrary economic acts of robbery by the white exploiters ("Black Man's Burden") and the whole system of so-called "Jim Crowism." Here, however, it is very important in connection with all these concrete cases of conflict to concentrate the attention of the Negro masses not so much to the general demands of mere equality, but much more to some of the revolutionary basic demands arising from the concrete situation.

The slogan of the right of self-determination occupies the central place in the liberation struggle of the Negro population in the Black Belt against the yoke of American imperialism, but this slogan, as we see it, must be carried out only in connection with two other basic demands. Thus, there are three basic demands to be kept in mind in the Black Belt, namely, the following:

1. *Confiscation of the landed property of the white landowners and capitalists for the benefit of the Negro farmers.* The landed property in the hands of the white American exploiters constitutes the most important material basis of the entire system of national oppression and serfdom of the Negroes in the Black Belt. More than three-quarters of all Negro farmers here are bound in actual serfdom to the farms and plantations of the white exploiters by the feudal system of "share cropping." Only on paper and not in practice are they freed from the yoke

of their former slavery. The same holds completely true for the great mass of black contract labourers; here the contract is only the capitalist expression of the chains of the old slavery, which even to-day are not infrequently applied in their natural iron form on the roads of the Black Belt (chain-gang work). These are the main forms of present Negro slavery in the Black Belt and no breaking of the chains of this slavery is possible without confiscating all the landed property of the white masters. Without this revolutionary measure, without the agrarian revolution, the right of self-determination of the Negro population would be only a Utopia, or at best would remain only on paper without changing in any way the actual enslavement.

2. *Establishment of the State Unity of the Black Belt.* At the present time this Negro zone—precisely for the purpose of facilitating national oppression—is artificially split up and divided into a number of various states which include distant localities having a majority of white population. If the right of self-determination of the Negroes is to be put into force, it is necessary wherever possible to bring together into one governmental unit all districts of the South where the majority of the settled population consists of Negroes. Within the limits of this state there will of course remain a fairly significant white minority which must submit to the right of self-determination of the Negro majority. There is no other possible way of carrying out in a democratic manner the right of self-determination of the Negroes. Every plan regarding the establishment of the Negro State with an exclusively Negro population in America (and, of course, still more exporting it to Africa) is nothing but an unreal and reactionary caricature of the fulfillment of the right of self-determination of the Negroes and every attempt to isolate and transport the Negroes would have the most damaging effect upon their interests; above all, it would violate the right of the Negro farmers in the Black Belt not only to their present residences and their land but also to the land owned by the white landlords and cultivated by Negro labour.

3. *Right of Self-Determination.* This means complete and unlimited right of the Negro majority to exercise governmental authority in the entire territory of the Black Belt, as well as to decide upon the relations between their territory

and other nations, particularly the United States. It would
not be right of self-determination in our sense of the word
if the Negroes in the Black Belt had the right of determination only in cases which concerned *exclusively* the Negroes
and did not affect the whites, because the most important
cases arising here are bound to affect the Negroes as well as
the whites. First of all, true right to self-determination
means that the Negro majority and not the white minority
in the entire territory of the administratively united Black
Belt exercises the right of administrating governmental, legislative and judicial authority. At the present time all this
power here is concentrated in the hands of the white bourgeoisie and landlords. It is they who appoint all officials, it
is they who dispose of public property, it is they who determine the taxes, it is they who govern and make the laws.
Therefore, *the overthrow of this class rule* in the Black Belt is
unconditionally necessary in the struggle for the Negroes'
right to self-determination. This, however, means at the
same time the overthrow of the yoke of American imperialism in the Black Belt on which the forces of the local white
bourgeoisie depend. Only in this way, only if the Negro
population of the Black Belt wins its freedom from
American imperialism even to the point of deciding itself
the relations between its country and other governments,
especially the United States, will it win real and complete
self-determination. One should demand from the beginning that no armed forces of American imperialism should
remain on the territory of the Black Belt.

7. As stated in the letter of the Polit. Secretariat of the E.C.C.I. of
March 16th, 1930, the Communists must "*unreservedly* carry on
a struggle" for the self-determination of the Negro population in
the Black Belt in accordance with what has been set forth above.
It is incorrect and harmful to interpret the Communist standpoint to mean that the Communists stand for the right of self-
determination of the Negroes only up to a certain point, but not
beyond this, for example, to the right of separation. It is also
incorrect to say that the Communists are so far only to carry on
propaganda or agitation for the right of self-determination, but
not to develop any activity to bring this about. No, it is of the
utmost importance for the Communist Party to reject any such
limitation of its struggle for this slogan. Even if the situation does

not yet warrant the raising of the question of uprising, one should not limit oneself at present to propaganda for the demand: "Right to self-determination," but should organize mass actions, such as demonstrations, strikes, tax-boycott-movements, etc.

Moreover, the Party cannot make its stand for this slogan dependent upon any conditions, even the condition that the proletariat has the hegemony in the national revolutionary Negro movement or that the majority of the Negroes in the Black Belt adopts the Soviet form (as Pepper demanded), etc. It goes without saying that the Communists in the Black Belt will and must try to win over all working elements of the Negroes, that is, the majority of the population, to their side and to convince them not only that they must win the right of self-determination, but also that they must make use of this right in accordance with the Communist programme. But this cannot be made a *condition* for the stand of the Communists in favor of the right of self-determination of the Negro population; if, or so long as the majority of this population wishes to handle the situation in the Black Belt in a different manner from that which we Communists would like, its complete right to self-determination must be recognized. This right we must defend as a free democratic right.

8. In general, the C.P. of the United States has kept to this correct line recently in its struggle for the right of self-determination of the Negroes even though this line—in some cases—has been unclearly or erroneously expressed. In particular some misunderstanding has arisen from the failure to make a clear distinction between the demand for "right of self-determination" and the demand for governmental separation, simply treating these two demands in the same way. However, these two demands are not identical. Complete right to self-determination includes also the right to governmental separation, but does not necessarily imply that the Negro population should *make use of this* right under all circumstances, that is, that it must actually separate or attempt to separate the Black Belt from the existing governmental federation with the United States. If it desires to separate it must be free to do so; but if it prefers to remain federated with the United States it must also be free to do that. This is the correct meaning of the idea of self-determination and it must be recognized quite independently of whether the United States are still a capitalist state or if a proletarian dictatorship has already been established there.

It is, however, another matter if it is not a case of the *right* of the oppressed nation concerned to separate or to maintain governmental contact, but if the question is treated on its merits; whether it is to work for state separation, whether it is to struggle *for this* or not. This is another question, on which the stand of the Communists must vary according to the concrete conditions. If the proletariat has come into power in the United States, the Communist Negroes will not come out for but *against* separation of the Negro Republic federation with the United States. But the *right* of the Negroes to governmental separation will be *unconditionally realized* by the Communist Party, it will unconditionally give the Negro population of the Black Belt freedom of choice even on this question. Only when the proletariat has come into power in the United States the Communists will carry on propaganda among the working masses of the Negro population against separation, in order to convince them that it is much better and in the interest of the Negro nation for the Black Belt to be a free republic, where the Negro majority has complete right of self-determination but remains governmentally federated with the great proletarian republic of the United States. The bourgeois counter-revolutionists on the other hand will then be interested in boosting the separation tendencies in the ranks of the various nationalities in order to utilize separatist nationalism as a barrier for the bourgeois counter-revolution against the consolidation of the proletarian dictatorship.

But the question at the present time is not this. As long as capitalism rules in the United States the Communists cannot come out against governmental separation of the Negro zone from the United States. They recognize that this separation from the imperialist United States would be preferable from the standpoint of the national interests of the Negro population, to their present oppressed state, and therefore, the Communists are ready at any time to offer all their support if only the working masses of the Negro population are ready to take up the struggle for governmental independence of the Black Belt. At the present time, however, the situation in the national struggle in the South is not such as to win mass support of the working Negroes for this separatist struggle; and it is not the task of the Communists to call upon them to separate without taking into consideration the existing situation and the desires of the Negro masses.

The situation in the Negro question of the United States, however, may undergo a radical change. It is even probable that the separatist efforts to obtain complete State independence of the Black Belt will gain ground among the Negro masses of the South in the near future. This is connected with the prospective sharpening of the national conflicts in the South, with the advance of the national revolutionary Negro movement and with the exceptionally brutal fascist aggressiveness of the white exploiters of the South, as well as with the support of this aggressiveness by the central government authority of the United States. In this sharpening of the situation in the South, Negro separatism will presumably increase, and the question of the independence of the Black Belt will become the question of the day. Then the Communist Party must also face this question and, if the circumstances seem favorable, must stand up with all strength and courage for the struggle to win independence and for the establishment of a Negro republic in the Black Belt.

9. The general relation of Communists to separatist tendencies among the Negroes, described above, cannot mean that Communists associate themselves at present, or generally speaking, during capitalism, indiscriminately and without criticism with all the separatist currents of the various bourgeois or petty-bourgeois Negro groups. For there is not only a national revolutionary, but also a reactionary Negro separatism, for instance, that represented by Garvey; his Utopia of an isolated Negro State (regardless if in Africa or America, if it is supposed to consist of Negroes only) pursues only the political aim of diverting the Negro masses from the real liberation struggle against American imperialism.

It would be a mistake to imagine that the right of self-determination slogan is a truly revolutionary slogan only in connection with the demand for complete separation. The question of power is decided not only through the demand of separation, but just as much through the demand of the right to decide the separation question and self-determination in general. A direct question of power is also the demand of confiscation of the land of the white exploiters in the South, as well as the demand of the Negroes that the entire Black Belt be amalgamated into a State unit.

Hereby, every single fundamental demand of the liberation struggle of the Negroes in the Black Belt is such that—if once thoroughly understood by the Negro masses and adopted as their slogan—it will lead them into the struggle for the overthrow of the power of the ruling bourgeoisie, which is impossible without such revolutionary struggle. One cannot deny that it is just possible for the Negro population of the Black Belt to win the right to self-determination already during capitalism; but it is perfectly clear and indubitable that this is possible only through successful revolutionary struggle for power against the American bourgeoisie, through wresting the Negroes' right to self-determination from the American imperialism. Thus, the slogan of right to self-determination is a real slogan of national rebellion which, to be considered as such, need not be supplemented by proclaiming struggle for the complete separation of the Negro zone, at least not at present. But it must be made perfectly clear to the Negro masses that the slogan "right to self-determination" includes the demand of full freedom for them to decide even the question of complete separation. "We demand freedom of separation, real right to self-determination"—wrote Lenin: "certainly not in order to 'recommend' separation, but on the contrary, in order to facilitate and accelerate the democratic rapprochement and unification of nations." For the same purpose, Lenin's Party, the C.P. of the Soviet Union, bestowed after its seizure of power on all the peoples hitherto oppressed by Russian Tsarism the full right to self-determination, including the right of complete separation, and achieved thereby its enormous successes with regard to the democratic rapprochement and voluntary unification of nations.

10. The slogan for the self-determination right and the other fundamental slogans of the Negro question in the Black Belt does not exclude but rather pre-supposes an energetic development of the struggle for concrete partial demands linked up with the daily needs and afflictions of wide masses of working Negroes. In order to avoid, in this connection, the danger of opportunist back-slidings, Communists must above all remember this:

   (a) The direct aims and partial demands around which a partial struggle develops are to be linked up in the course of the struggle with the revolutionary fundamental slogans brought up by the question of power, in a popular manner corresponding to the mood of the masses. (Confiscation of the big land-holdings, establishment of governmental unity of the Black Belt, right of self-determination of the Negro population in the Black Belt.) Bourgeois-socialist tendencies to oppose such a revolutionary widening and deepening of the fighting demands must be fought.

(b) One should not venture to draw up a complete programme of some kind or a system of "positive" partial demands. Such programmes on the part of petty-bourgeois politicians should be exposed as attempts to divert the masses from the necessary hard struggles by fostering reformist and democratic illusions among them. Every positive partial demand which might crop up is to be considered from the viewpoint of whether it is in keeping with our revolutionary fundamental slogans, or whether it is of a reformist or reactionary tendency. Every kind of national oppression which arouses the indignation of the Negro masses can be used as a suitable point of departure for the development of partial struggles, during which the abolition of such oppression, as well as their prevention through revolutionary struggle against the ruling exploiting dictatorship must be demanded.

(c) Everything should be done to bring wide masses of Negroes into these partial struggles—this is important—and not to carry the various partial demands to such an ultra-radical point, that the mass of working Negroes are no longer able to recognize them as *their own*. Without a real mobilisation of the mass-movements—in spite of the sabotage of the bourgeois reformist Negro politicians—even the best Communist partial demands get hung up. On the other hand, even some relatively insignificant acts of the Ku-Klux-Klan bandits in the Black Belt can become the occasion of important political movements, provided the Communists are able to organise the resistance of the indignant Negro masses. In such cases, mass movements of this kind can easily develop into real rebellion. This rests on the fact that—as Lenin said— "Every act of national oppression calls forth resistance on the part of the masses of the population, and the tendency of every act of resistance on the part of oppressed peoples is the national uprising."

(d) Communists must fight in the *forefront* of the national-liberation movement and must do their utmost for the progress of this mass movement and its revolutionisation. Negro Communists must *clearly dissociate* themselves from all bourgeois currents in the Negro movement, must indefatigably oppose the spread of the influence of the bourgeois groups on the working Negroes, and in dealing with them must apply the Communist tactic laid down by the Sixth C.I. Congress with regard to the colonial question, in order to guarantee the *hegemony of the Negro proletariat* in the national liberation movement of the Negro population, and to co-ordinate wide masses of the Negro peasantry in a steady fighting alliance with the proletariat.

(e) One must work with the utmost energy for the establishment and consolidation of *Communist Party organisations and* revolutionary *trade unions* in the South. Furthermore, immediate measures must be taken for the organisation of proletarian and peasant *self-defense* of whites and blacks against the Ku-Klux-Klan; for this purpose, the C.P. is to give further instructions.

11. It is particularly incumbent on Negro Communists to criticize consistently the half-heartedness and hesitations of the petty-bourgeois national-revolutionary Negro leaders in the liberation struggle of the Black Belt, exposing them before the masses. All national reformist currents as, for instance, Garveyism, which are an obstacle to the revolutionisation of the Negro masses, must be fought systematically and with the utmost energy. Simultaneously, Negro Communists must carry on among the Negro masses an energetic struggle against nationalist moods directed indiscriminately against all whites, workers as well as capitalists, Communists, as well as imperialists. Their constant call to the Negro masses must be: *revolutionary struggle against the ruling white bourgeoisie, through a fighting alliance with the revolutionary white proletariat!* Negro Communists must indefatigably explain to the mass of the Negro population that even if many white workers in America are still infected with Negrophobia, the American proletariat, as a class, which owing to its struggle against the American bourgeoisie represents the only truly revolutionary class, will be the only real mainstay of Negro liberation. In as far as successes in the national-revolutionary struggle of the Negro population of the South for its right to self-determination are already possible under capitalism, they can be achieved only if this struggle is effectively supported by proletarian mass actions on a large scale in the other parts of the United States. But it is also clear that "only a victorious proletarian revolution will *finally* decide the agrarian question and the national question in the South of the United States, in the interest of the predominating

mass of the Negro population of the country." (Colonial Theses of the Sixth World Congress.)

12. The struggle regarding the Negro question in the North must be linked up with the liberation struggle in the South, in order to endow the Negro movement throughout the United States with the necessary effective strength. After all, in the North as well as in the South, it is a question of the real emancipation of the American Negroes which has in fact never taken place before. The Communist Party of the United States must bring into play its entire revolutionary energy in order to mobilize the widest possible masses of the white and black proletariat of the United States, not by words, but by deeds, for real effective support of the struggle for the liberation of the Negroes. Enslavement of the Negroes is one of the most important foundations of the imperialist dictatorship of U.S.A. capitalism. The more American imperialism fastens its yoke on the millions strong Negro masses, the more must the Communist Party develop the mass struggle for Negro emancipation, and the better use it must make of all conflicts which arise out of national differences, as an incentive for revolutionary mass actions against the bourgeoisie. This is as much in the direct interest of the proletarian revolution in America. Whether the rebellion of the Negroes is to be the outcome of a general revolutionary situation in the United States, whether it is to originate in the whirlpool of decisive fights for power by the working-class, for proletarian dictatorship, or whether on the contrary, the Negro rebellion will be the prelude of gigantic struggles for power by the American proletariat, cannot be foretold now. But in either contingency, it is essential for the Communist Party *to make an energetic beginning already now* with the organisation of *joint mass struggles* of white and black workers against Negro oppression. This alone will enable us to get rid of the bourgeois white chauvinism which is polluting the ranks of the white workers of America, to overcome the distrust of the Negro masses caused by the inhuman barbarous Negro slave traffic still carried on by the American bourgeoisie—in as far as it is directed even against all white workers—and to win over to our side these millions of Negroes as active fellow fighters in the struggle for the overthrow of bourgeois power throughout America.

Selected Bibliography

Anderson, Carol. "Bleached Souls and Red Negroes: the NAACP and Black Communists in the Early Cold War, 1948–1952." In *The Achievement of American Liberalism: The New Deal and Its Legacies*, edited by William Henry Chafe. New York: Columbia University Press, 2003.

Allen, James S. *Negro Liberation*. New York: International Publishers, 1938.

Baldwin, Kate A. *Beyond the Color Line and the Iron Curtain: Reading Encounters between Black and Red, 1922–1963*. Durham, NC: Duke University Press, 2002.

Berland, Oscar. "The Communist Perspective on the 'Negro Question' in America, 1919–1931." *Science and Society* 63 & 64, nos. 4 and 2 (Winter-Summer 1999–2000).

———. "Nasanov and the Comintern's American Negro Program." *Science and Society* 65, no. 2 (2001).

Blakely, Allison. *Russia and the Negro: Blacks in Russian History and Thought*. Washington, DC: Howard University Press, 1986.

Bornet, Vaughn D. "Historical Scholarship, Communism, and the Negro." *The Journal of Negro History* 37, no. 3 (July 1952).

Campbell, Susan. "'Black Bolsheviks' and Recognition of African-America's Right to Self-Determination by the Communist Party U.S.A." *Science and Society* 58, no. 4 (1994/95).

Carter, Dan T. *Scottsboro: A Tragedy of the American South*. Baton Rouge: Louisiana State University Press, 1979.

Davis, Benjamin J. *Communist Councilman from Harlem: Autobiographical Notes Written in a Federal Penitentiary*. New York: International Publishers, 1969.

Edwards, Brent Hayes. "Dossier on Black Radicalism: Introduction: The Autonomy of Black Radicalism." *Social Text* 19, no. 2 (2001).

Eversole, Theodore W. "Benjamin J. Davis, Jr. (1903–1964): From Republican Atlanta Lawyer to Harlem Communist Councilman." *Journal of the Afro-American Historical and Genealogical Society* 8, no. 1 (1987).

Foner, Philip Sheldon. *American Socialism and Black Americans from the Age of Jackson to World War II*. Westport, CT: Greenwood Press, 1977.

———, and James S. Allen, eds. *American Communism and Black Americans: A Documentary History, 1919–1929*. Philadelphia: Temple University Press, 1987.

———, and Herbert Shapiro, eds. *American Communism and Black Americans: A Documentary History, 1930–1934*. Philadelphia: Temple University Press, 1991.

Ford, James W. *The Negro and the Democratic Front*. New York: International Publishers, 1938.

Gardner, John L. "African Americans in the Soviet Union in the 1920s and 1930s: The Development of Transcontinental Protest." *Western Journal of Black Studies* 23, no. 3 (1999).

Goldfield, Michael. "The Decline of the Communist Party and the Black Question in the U.S.: Harry Haywood's Black Bolshevik." *Review of Radical Political Economics* 12, no. 1 (1980).

Goodman, James E. *Stories of Scottsboro*. New York: Pantheon Books, 1994.

Grigsby, Daryl Russell. *For the People: Black Socialists in the United States, Africa, and the Caribbean*. San Diego: Asante Publications, 1987.

Haywood, Harry. *The Road to Negro Liberation: The Tasks of the Communist Party in Winning Working Class Leadership of the Negro Liberation Struggles, and the Fight against Reactionary Nationalist-Reformist Movements among the Negro People*. New York: Workers Library, 1934.

———. *Black Bolshevik: Autobiography of an Afro-American Communist*. Chicago: Liberator Press, 1978.

Hill, Robert A. "Racial and Radical: Cyril V. Briggs, *The Crusader* Magazine, and the African Blood Brotherhood, 1918–1922." In *The Crusader*. New York: Garland., 1987.

Hooker, James R. *Black Revolutionary: George Padmore's Path from Communism to Pan-Africanism*. New York: Praeger, 1967.

Horne, Gerald. *Black Liberation/Red Scare: Ben Davis and the Communist Party*. Newark, DE: University of Delaware Press, 1993.

———. *Studies in Black: Progressive Views and Reviews of the African-American Experience*. Dubuque, IA: Kendall/Hunt, 1992.

———. "The Red and the Black: The Communist Party and African-Americans in Historical Perspective." In *New Studies in the Politics and*

Culture of U.S. Communism, edited by Michael E. Brown, Randy Martin, Frank Rosengarten, and George Snedeker. New York: Monthly Review Press, 1993.

Howard, Walter T. B. D. *Amis, African American Radical: A Short Anthology of Writings and Speeches*. Lanham, MD: University Press of America, 2007.

Hutchinson, Earl Ofari. *Blacks and Reds: Race and Class in Conflict, 1919–1990*. East Lansing: Michigan State University Press, 1995.

Jackson, James E. *Revolutionary Tracings*. New York: International Publishers, 1974.

James, Winston. *Holding Aloft the Banner of Ethiopia: Caribbean Radicalism in Early Twentieth-Century America*. London, New York: Verso, 1998.

Johanningsmeier, Edward. "Communists and Black Freedom Movements in South Africa and the U.S.: 1919–1950." *Journal of Southern African Studies* 30, no. 1 (March 2004).

Kanet, Roger. "The Comintern and the 'Negro Question': Communist Policy in the United States and Africa, 1921–1941." *Survey* [U.K.] 19, no. 4 (Autumn 1973).

Kelley, Robin D. G. *Hammer and Hoe: Alabama Communists during the Great Depression* Chapel Hill: University of North Carolina Press, 1984.

———. *Race Rebels: Culture, Politics, and the Black Working Class*. New York and Toronto: Free Press and Maxwell Macmillan, 1994.

———. "But a Local Phase of World Problem: Black History's Global Vision, 1883–1950." *Journal of American History* 86, no. 3 (December 1999).

Klehr, Harvey, and William Tompson. "Self-Determination in the Black Belt: Origins of a Communist Policy." *Labor History* 30, no. 3 (Summer 1989).

Kornweibel, Theodore, Jr. *"Seeing Red": Federal Campaign against Black Militancy, 1919–1925*. Bloomington: Indiana University Press, 1998.

Klore, Joe. "Harlem's Communist Councilman, Ben Davis Jr." *Political Affairs* 81, no. 2 (2002).

Kosa, John, and Clyde. Z. Nunn. "Race, Deprivation and Attitude Toward Communism." *Phylon* 25, no. 4 (1964).

McClellan, Woodford. "Africans and Black Americans in the Comintern Schools, 1925–1934." *International Journal of African Historical Studies* 26, no. 2 (1993).

Marable, Manning. "Why Black Americans Are Not Socialists." In *Socialist Perspectives*, edited by Phyllis Jacobson and Julius Jacobson, assisted by Petr Abovin-Egides. Princeton, NJ: Karz-Cohl, 1983.

Markowitz, Norman. "Benjamin Davis, Jr.: Centennial, 1903–2003." *Political Affairs* 82, no. 2 (February 2003).

Martin, Charles H. "The International Labor Defense and Black Americans." *Labor History* 26, no. 2 (Spring 1985).

Miller, James A., Susan D. Pennybacker, and Eve Rosenhaft. "Mother Ada Wright and the International Campaign to Free the Scottsboro Boys." *American Historical Review* 106, no. 2 (April 2001).

Murray, Hugh T., Jr.. "The NAACP versus the Communist Party: The Scottsboro Rape Cases, 1931–1932." *Phylon* 28, no. 3 (1967).

———. "Aspects of the Scottsboro Campaign." *Science and Society* 35, no. 2 (Summer 1971).

———. "Changing America and the Changing Image of Scottsboro." *Phylon*, 38, no. 1 (1977).

Naison, Mark. "Marxism and Black Radicalism in America: Notes on a Long (and Continuing) Journey." *Radical America* 5, no. 3 (May–June 1971).

———. "Communism and Black Nationalism in the Depression: The Case of Harlem." *Journal of Ethnic Studies* 2, no. 2 (Summer 1974).

———. "The Communist Party in Harlem: 1928–1936." PhD diss., Columbia University, 1976.

———. "The Communist Party in Harlem in the Early Depression Years: A Case Study in the Reinterpretation of American Communism." *Radical History Review*, no. 3 (Fall 1976).

———. "Harlem Communists and the Politics of Black Protest." *Marxist Perspectives* 1, no. 3 (Fall 1978).

———. "Historical Notes on Blacks and American Communism: The Harlem Experience." *Science and Society* 42, no. 3 (Fall 1978).

———. *Communists in Harlem during the Depression.* Urbana: University of Illinois Press, 1983.

Nolan, William Anthony. *Communism versus the Negro.* Chicago: H. Regnery Company, 1951.

Parascandola, Louis J. "Cyril Briggs and the African Blood Brotherhood: A Radical Counterpoint to Progressivism," *New York Life and History* (January 2006).

Patterson, William L. *The Man Who Cried Genocide: An Autobiography.* New York: International Publishers, 1971.

Record, Wilson. "American Racial Ideologies and Organizations in Transition." *Phylon* 26, no. 4 (1965).

———. *The Negro and the Communist Party.* Chapel Hill: University of North Carolina Press, 1951.

———. "The Development of the Communist Position on the Negro Question in the United States." *Phylon* 19, no. 3 (Fall 1958).

———. *Race and Radicalism: The NAACP and the Communist Party in Conflict.* Ithaca, NY: Cornell University Press, 1964.

Rywkin, Michael. "Black Americans: A Race or Nationality? Some Communist Viewpoints." *Canadian Review of Studies in Nationalism* 3, no. 1 (1975).

Solomon, Mark. "Red and Black: Negroes and Communism, 1929–1932." PhD diss., Harvard University, 1972.

————. *Red and Black: Communism and Afro-Americans, 1929–1935.* New York: Garland, 1988.

————. *The Cry Was Unity: Communists and African Americans, 1917–36.* Jackson: University Press of Mississippi, 1998.

Spark, Clare. "Race, Caste, or Class? The Bunche-Myrdal Dispute Over an American Dilemma." *International Journal of Politics, Culture, and Society* 14, no. 3 (Spring 2001).

Sullivan, William C. "Communism and the American Negro." *Religion in Life* 37, no. 4 (1968).

Thomas, Theman. "Cyril Briggs and the African Blood Brotherhood: Another Radical View of Race and Class during the 1920s," PhD diss., University of California, Santa Barbara, 1981.

Thomas, Tony. "Black Nationalism and Confused Marxists." *Black Scholar* 4, no. 1 (1972).

Turner, W. Burghardt, and Joyce Moore Turner, eds., *Richard B. Moore, Caribbean Militant in Harlem: Collected Writings, 1920–1972.* Bloomington: University of Indiana Press, 1989.

Van West, Carroll. "Perpetuating the Myth of America: Scottsboro and Its Interpreters." *South Atlantic Quarterly* 80 (1981).

Van Zanter, John W. "Communist Theory and the American Negro Question." *Review of Politics* 29, no. 4 (1967).

Wald, Alan. "New Black Radical Scholarship." *Against the Current*, no. 108 (January–February 2004).

————. "The U.S. Left and Anti-Racism." In *Black Liberation and the American Dream: The Struggle for Racial and Economic Justice: Analysis, Strategy, Readings,* edited by Paul Le Blanc. Amherst, NY: Humanity Books, 2003.

Wexley, John. "They Shall Not Die." In *Proletarian Literature in the United States: An Anthology,* edited by Granville Hicks and Joseph Freeman. New York: International Publishers, 1935.

Williams, Henry. *Black Response to the American Left: 1917–1929.* Princeton, NJ: Princeton University, 1973.

Williams, Lynn Barstis. "Images of Scottsboro." *Southern Cultures* 6, no. 1 (2000).

Wynn, Daniel Webster. *The NAACP versus Negro Revolutionary Protest: A Comparative Study of the Effectiveness of Each Movement.* New York: Exposition Press, 1955.

Index

Semi-feudal oppression, 160
Senate, 23
Separatist nationalism, 178
Share cropping, 160, 174
Sharecroppers, 7, 92, 105, 134
Sheriff(s), 69, 70, 91, 132, 134, 138, 140
Sheriff J. Street Sandlin, 19, 132, 134, 144
Shooting, 64, 75, 132
Shop, 111
Shop organization, 97
Slave(s), 4, 12, 38, 39, 40, 60, 87, 88, 90, 95, 142, 143, 145, 150, 151, 156, 160, 161, 167, 169, 170, 171
Slave whipping, 170
Slavery, 4, 39, 45, 60, 66, 82, 88, 117, 119, 150, 167, 168, 169, 175
Social antagonism, 168
Social equality, 4, 100, 168
Social fascists, 62
Social insurance, 82
Socialism, 20, 23, 93
Socialist(s), 5, 6, 17, 23, 24, 25, 66, 67, 89, 93, 95, 96, 105, 108, 165, 167, 171
Socialist Party, 5, 6, 15, 23, 93, 95, 108
Socialist Revolution, 167
Solidarity, 4, 8, 46, 48, 63, 65, 77, 78, 96, 102, 104, 111, 127, 128, 145, 164, 172
South, 2, 6, 8, 9, 14, 19, 21, 22, 23, 27, 29, 33, 37, 41, 46, 55, 57, 58, 62, 71, 92, 98, 102, 107, 109, 115, 137, 141, 147, 150, 159, 160, 163, 167, 168, 169, 170, 172, 173, 175, 178, 179
Southern, 4, 7, 11, 15, 20, 27, 29, 30, 31, 35, 36, 41, 42, 43, 45, 79, 87, 89, 92, 99, 124, 133, 134, 142, 143, 159, 161, 168
South Africa, 23, 46, 63, 64, 66, 161
Southern boss lynchers, 42, 43
Southern cities, 26
Southern courts, 42
Southern ruling class, 29, 30, 92, 134
Southern states, 45, 159, 161
Soviet Union, 12, 24, 43, 45, 49, 62, 67, 104, 147, 156
Steel bosses, 42

Strike(s), 6, 8, 9, 16, 62, 64, 71, 82, 107, 111, 121, 134, 164, 172

Tampa, Fl., 36, 105, 128
Tenant(s), 7, 8, 34, 62, 160, 165, 167, 169
Tennessee, 1, 11
Terror, 4, 9, 32, 36, 38, 40, 44, 48, 52, 53, 59, 62, 63, 66, 67, 71, 75, 77, 80, 81, 83, 91, 92, 93, 96, 98, 100, 103, 104, 105, 108, 112, 122, 127, 130
Terrorism, 14, 32
Terrorist(s), 71
Texas, 8, 70, 88
Thomas, Norman, 15
Toilers, 14, 60, 61, 62, 63, 64, 65, 66, 69, 71, 86, 88, 89, 90, 94, 95, 96, 97, 112, 170
Toiling masses, 62, 104, 105, 160, 167
Torture, 4, 130, 133, 143
Trade Union Educational League (TUEL), 163

Uncle Tom leaders, 39, 40, 43
Unemployed, 35, 37, 69, 70, 75, 82, 97, 98, 106, 110, 112, 128, 137
Unemployed Councils, 35
Unemployment, 35, 37, 44, 48, 53, 62, 64, 69, 81, 82, 104, 157
Unemployment relief, 9, 53
Union(s), 5, 7, 25, 35, 53, 106, 148, 162, 163, 170, 172
United front, 17, 18, 20, 27, 29, 38, 40, 43, 49, 51, 54, 62, 53, 67, 83, 87, 95, 96, 97, 98, 105, 106, 114, 117, 118, 120, 153, 166
United Front Scottsboro Defense Committee, 41
United States, 3, 4, 5, 6, 7, 11, 12, 15, 17, 20, 21, 23, 28, 29, 31, 33, 36, 38, 41, 45, 48, 61, 62, 63, 64, 67, 68, 74, 76, 77, 78, 83, 84, 86, 102, 103, 104, 108, 112, 131, 132, 139, 141, 147, 156, 157, 159, 161, 167, 168, 169, 170, 171, 172, 173, 176, 177, 178, 179
Universal Negro Improvement Association, 7, 29, 62

Walter T. Howard is Professor of American History at Bloomsburg Universit, in northeastern Pennsylvania. He is the editor of *B.D. Amis, African American Radical: A Short Anthology of Writings and Speeches* and the author of *Lynchings: Extralegal Violence in Florida during the 1930s.*